THE
REAL ESTATE
WHOLESALING
BIBLE

THE
REAL ESTATE
WHOLESALING
BIBLE

The Fastest, Easiest Way to Get Started in
Real Estate Investing

THAN MERRILL

WILEY

Library of Congress Cataloging-in-Publication Data:

Merrill, Than.
    The Real Estate Wholesaling Bible: The Fastest, Easiest Way to Get Started in Real Estate Investing/Than Merrill.
        ISBN: 978-1-118-80752-1 (pbk.); ISBN 978-1-118-90041-3 (ebk);
        ISBN: 978-1-118-90039-0 (ebk)
        1. Real estate investment.   I. Title.
    HD1382.5
    332.63'24—dc23

                                                                    2014002385

Printed in the United States of America
SKY10027330_052721

Contents

Introduction

Welcome to the world of real estate wholesaling. This book was written to help you understand a very appealing facet of the real estate investing industry and to help you succeed as a real estate wholesaler. In the pages to follow, you will discover the opportunities and rewards, as well as the risks and challenges, of wholesaling real estate.

If you are new to wholesaling, this book will provide you a comprehensive outline and roadmap of how to get started and succeed. You will also want to use this book as a reference guide to refer back to as you navigate through your first few wholesale transactions.

If you are already actively wholesaling, this book will help propel you to the next level of achievement. I will discuss and uncover many different ways to automate your real estate investing efforts and build a business that is not completely dependent on you as the business owner. Many real estate investors' sense of success comes from the process of building a business that "works" or is "profitable." From my point of view, having a business that works is not enough. I believe success is when your real estate investment wholesaling business is not only profitable, but also gives you the time to enjoy your life and fulfill your passions and dreams. I believe success is defined as having a turnkey, systems-dependent business that serves as a vehicle for all the people it touches: the owners, the employees, and the community. Without a doubt, both beginning and advanced investors alike will benefit from implementing the lessons learned in this book.

Over a decade ago, I picked up my first real estate investing book. That book was a catalyst for major change in my own life and I want this book to be the catalyst for you, the next generation of real estate investor. Study hard. Keep an open mind. And take charge of your financial destiny once and for all.

THE SHRINKING MIDDLE CLASS IN AMERICA

One of the reasons I believe you should take a much greater interest in controlling your financial destiny is to ensure you don't fall victim to the shrinking middle class in America.

Unfortunately, the middle class in the United States is being systematically destroyed and nobody is doing much to stop it. The number of middle-class families who earn between $40,000 and $200,000 a year is shrinking at an alarming rate. Median household income levels have fallen, jobs are being sent overseas, debt burdens have soared to new heights, and millions of formerly middle-class Americans have fallen below the poverty level.

Once upon a time, a college degree was a ticket to the middle class; today's college graduates are having an increasingly hard time finding work. Here are some scary facts about the shrinking middle class in America:

- Last year, an astounding 53 percent of all U.S. college graduates under the age of 25 were either unemployed or underemployed.[1]
- According to one survey, 77 percent of all Americans are now living paycheck to paycheck at least part of the time.[2]
- While debt loads for middle-class families are going up, the net worth of those same families is going down. According to the Federal Reserve, the median net worth of families in the United States declined "from $126,400 in 2007 to $77,300 in 2010."[3]
- Each year, the average American must work 107 days just to make enough money to pay local, state, and federal taxes.[4]
- According to the Employee Benefit Research Institute, 46 percent of all American workers have less than $10,000 saved for retirement, and 29 percent of all American workers have less than $1,000 saved for retirement.[5]
- According to the Economic Policy Institute, America is losing half a million jobs to China every single year.[6]
- Today, 40 percent of all Americans have $500 or less in savings.[7]

---

[1] http://theeconomiccollapseblog.com/archives/53-percent-of-all-young-college-graduates-in-america-are-either-unemployed-or-underemployed

[2] http://thetruthwins.com/archives/77-percent-of-all-americans-live-paycheck-to-paycheck-at-least-part-of-the-time

[3] www.washingtonpost.com/business/economy/fed-americans-wealth-dropped-40-percent/2012/06/11/gJQAlIsCVV_story.html

[4] http://money.cnn.com/2012/04/02/pf/taxes/tax-freedom-day/index.htm?iid=Lead

[5] www.ebri.org/pdf/surveys/rcs/2011/FS2_RCS11_Prepare_FINAL1.pdf

[6] http://economyincrisis.org/content/trade-deficit-china-could-cost-half-million-jobs

[7] http://philadelphia.cbslocal.com/2012/10/19/survey-40-percent-of-americans-have-500-or-less-in-savings/

Statistics tell us that for the first time in history you may not be better off than your parents. People are unfortunately worrying about survival rather than chasing their goals and dreams. We are rapidly being transformed from a country of middle-class citizens into a country of government dependents.

What you are about to learn in this book can help you avoid becoming a statistic. Real estate has long been America's number-one wealth builder. It is a tried-and-true path to building wealth and has transformed the lives of millions of regular, everyday people.

HOW I GOT STARTED INVESTING IN REAL ESTATE

Twelve years ago, at the age of 23, I was a rookie playing for the Chicago Bears in the National Football League. In the offseason I had what I thought was a great idea and I decided I was going to start a Mexican restaurant with the money I had saved.

Yes, I was officially an entrepreneur. Unfortunately, at the time, with very little business education behind me, I can't say I was necessarily a good one. Seriously, who starts a Mexican restaurant while he is still playing in the NFL in the prime of his life? I distinctly remember warming up before a game against the Minnesota Vikings and getting a call before kickoff from Alfredo, the manager of my restaurant, asking me what to do because we were out of tortillas.

I started the restaurant because I thought having a good, entrepreneurial idea was enough to make serious money in business. Some people call this an "entrepreneurial seizure." In my case it was more of an "entrepreneurial burp."

After injuring my knee and then being released from the NFL (for being too darn fast), I poured all my entrepreneurial energy into the restaurant. I was working 12- to 14-hour days and hating every second of it. I figured out very quickly that it was a tough business and at the time I hadn't invested enough in my education to make it successful.

There are moments in everyone's life that have the power to spark massive change—moments that define your future and the path you ultimately choose to take. Not living up to the personal goals I had set for myself in the NFL and then having my entrepreneurial dream turn into a nightmare was too much for me to handle. After close to two years of running the restaurant I realized I didn't have a passion for the business and I knew I had to make a change—a *massive* change.

I immediately started reading books about something I had always had a passion for: real estate. I had no prior knowledge, had never taken a class, and had nobody to ask for advice regarding how to invest, but it didn't matter. I knew I could find the answers and people to learn from if I was determined enough. I also knew I had to spend time learning about the industry before I jumped in headfirst. I was determined not to make the same mistake and get into an industry without the proper education.

As a result, I devoured books and courses and started attending many different real estate investing seminars. After months of studying, I decided it was time to get off the sidelines, take action, and purchase a few properties. I also knew that I would continue my education as I acquired more properties and that I was never going to stop learning as my investment portfolio grew. Thus, my personal journey into the real estate investing world began.

Even though I was still very new to the industry, I quickly realized its potential. I subsequently decided to partner with Paul Esajian, one of my good childhood friends, and Konrad Sopielnikow, one of my old football teammates from Yale University.

To make ends meet, I was still working long hours in my restaurant, wearing what seemed like 15 different hats at once. In the early morning and on the weekends, I'd put on my real estate hat and look at properties. After purchasing a few rental properties, my partners and I decided it was time to start flipping real estate so we could grow our real estate investing business.

WHY WE DECIDED TO START WHOLESALING

After purchasing a few rental properties we then acquired two properties we started rehabbing to flip. The problem was we were pretty much out of capital, yet we still kept finding other good real estate deals.

This is when we discovered how valuable learning how to wholesale real estate could be. With the first two properties we wholesaled we made over $50,000. The two transactions took just under two months to structure and it helped us launch our real estate investing careers.

Wholesaling provided the gasoline we needed to really grow what started out as a hobby and quickly became a business. Over the past 10 years of investing in real estate, wholesaling has been a very large part of our real estate investing business.

Over the years, we have utilized wholesaling in various ways in our real estate business:

- Whenever we need money for other real estate deals we wholesale properties to create some of that capital.

- If we run across a real estate deal that is not in our backyard, we usually prefer to wholesale the property to another investor.
- Whenever we feel we have too many properties we are rehabbing we always wholesale other real estate deals that we find to other investors.
- If we are working on larger redevelopment projects, we will often choose to wholesale other deals that come our way.
- We buy a lot of properties from other wholesalers and it has been one of our better sources for properties we have fixed and flipped.
- We buy a lot of properties from other wholesalers that we keep and turn into rental properties that create cash flow.

In the next chapter I will share with you some of the top benefits of learning to wholesale real estate and how you can utilize it in your investment game plan.

I have also had the unique opportunity to coach thousands of real estate investors around the country. Through our seminars and coaching program, we have changed the lives of thousands of real estate investors by giving them a sound business model to follow. As a coach I have come to realize that the majority of our most successful investor students have also made wholesaling a large part of what they do as real estate investors.

Based on my personal experience and the experience of coaching thousands of other investors, I strongly believe that wholesaling should be a part of what you do as a real estate investor if you want to reach your financial goals. If you are just getting started, it can be a great way to earn some conservative profits in a relatively quick time frame. If you are more experienced, I believe it can really help you grow your investing efforts that much quicker.

SET SKEPTICISM ASIDE—IT WILL HOLD YOU BACK

As an experienced real estate investor and someone intimately familiar with how investors think, I know that some people have some skepticism about wholesaling or about real estate investing in general. Often people think that it's different for them or that it won't work where they live.

I've heard countless excuses why this won't work in particular cities or with certain property types. However, after coaching countless investors, I know wholesaling—coupled with our approach and systems—can work seamlessly in every market and with every property type.

Yes, there are stronger real estate markets than others. However, it's less about what the market is doing and more about what you are doing within the market. No matter where you live, there are people who are making money in real estate. Likewise, in every market there are people who are wholesaling real estate to other investors.

To benefit from this book, you have to first clear away all the misconceptions that somehow your situation is different. I believe a small amount of skepticism is healthy and can help people make better decisions. However, an overdose of skepticism can blind people and cause them to miss really good legitimate wealth-building opportunities.

I have seen plenty of intelligent and ambitious people who have missed great opportunities because they started listening to overly skeptical cynics who repeatedly tell them why something won't work. I believe one of the worst things you can do is listen to and take advice from people who are not where you want to be financially. The problem is the cynic is often a friend or a close family member. Some may subconsciously not want to see you succeed. However, the majority of cynics actually believe they are trying to protect you from getting hurt, when in reality they are holding you back from success.

Cynics will be more likely to tell you why they believe something won't work. If you let them influence you, you will end up doing nothing in real estate. What you believe to be true eventually ends up becoming your reality. Think about it. It's a lot easier to say why something won't work because it requires no effort. It's easier to give up in comparison to throwing your hat in the ring and trying to succeed.

Instead of taking the easy route, which is to do nothing, challenge the way you might be thinking and ask yourself how you can make this work. Wholesaling real estate is not a new concept. Investors have been wholesaling real estate for decades and it will continue to be an opportunity for decades to come.

IS THIS BOOK FOR YOU?

This book was written for intelligent, hardworking, rational people who have a strong desire to change their lives financially through real estate. If you're looking for a *magic formula* that is instantly going to change your entire life, then this book is *not* for you. This book was written to give you a very strong foundation and understanding of how wholesaling works. However, it will require that you dedicate a lot of time, energy, and focus to learning how wholesaling works. Then, you will have to get up off your duff and implement what you have learned, knowing that you could fail. In fact, most people fail before they ever succeed.

If you're willing to do the work, if you continue to educate yourself as you invest, if you look for a mentor to help guide you, and if you are willing to dedicate the time, then wholesaling real estate can change your life. If you have what it takes, wholesaling real estate can allow you to live a life others only dream about. It can give you the freedom to do what you want, when you want, with whomever you want. It will give you the freedom to enjoy life's finer pleasures. It will allow you to not just create a business, but leave a legacy.

THE CATALYST TO A BETTER LIFE

Learning how to wholesale was a defining moment in my entrepreneurial life. I hope this book has the same impact on you as you dive deeper and learn the mechanics of how to wholesale and, ultimately, how to build a wholesaling business that runs without you.

The road to achieving success as a real estate wholesaler is a hard one. You will have days when you want to quit and will begin to think that selling insurance doesn't sound so bad. Don't give in. Don't give up. Trust me. Learning how to invest in real estate has the power to change your life forever.

Over the years, we have helped thousands of real estate investors get a successful start with our systems and coaching programs. To learn more about how we can help you on your own road to real estate success, visit us online at www .FortuneBuildersMastery.com.

Enjoy the journey.

CHAPTER 1

Wholesaling Overview

What's in It for You?

Nothing can be loved or hated unless it is first known.

—LEONARDO DAVINCI

Over 80 percent of Americans do not have what they consider to be their dream job. Worse, many Americans take jobs they despise just so that they can make ends meet. That's an unfortunate way to live life. And it's an unnecessary one. Real estate investing can be a way out of this dilemma for people who are willing to put in the necessary time to educate themselves. Even if you aren't interested in investing in real estate on a full-time basis, it still has the power to be a means to an end.

I can't even begin to imagine what my life would be like if I hadn't made the decision to pick up that first real estate investing book over a decade ago. Real estate is my life's work, and I take great pride in calling myself a real estate investor. Even if investing isn't your dream job, it can give you the financial freedom you need to spend more time pursuing your higher calling. However you look at it, you have something to gain from learning to invest in real estate as a wholesaler.

THE BENEFITS OF LEARNING HOW TO WHOLESALE REAL ESTATE

As you are probably aware, there are numerous facets within the real estate investing industry. There are also benefits and risks associated with each of these facets, or *niches*, of real estate.

Wholesaling is a short-term real estate investment strategy that can be utilized to create quick profits. Essentially, you are finding properties that can be purchased at significantly below market value that you will control through the use of a *purchase and sale agreement*. Then while in contract, or shortly after you close on the property, you will locate a buyer who is willing to purchase your contract, or the property, from you for a profit.

Many investors focus only on wholesaling. Likewise, you will find wholesalers in every local real estate market around the country. However, most real estate investors who wholesale also invest in real estate in other ways as well. The key is to understand the benefits of wholesaling, how to perform wholesale transactions, and where it fits in your overall real estate wealth-building plan. Then you can choose what properties will be best to wholesale versus utilizing other exit strategies.

Benefit #1: Profits Can Be Quick

One of the reasons wholesaling is so attractive to many new investors is due to the speed with which you can find a property, put it under contract, find a buyer, and earn a profit from the transaction. I don't know of any quicker way to make a profit in real estate than wholesaling.

Typically, residential transactions take from three to six weeks to complete once you have the property under contract. Of course, there are deals that will happen quicker; however, they are the exception rather than the norm. Either way, you will not find any other facet of real estate where you can earn a profit in this short of a time period.

This makes it ideal for people who are relatively new to investing in real estate. It also makes it a perfect strategy for anybody who is working a full-time job, but still wants to get started and dip a toe in the market.

Once you have marketing campaigns in place, the knowledge to complete complicated transactions, and systems to help you evaluate deals and manage all the information, the transactions can happen relatively quickly. Obviously, the more knowledge you acquire and the better your systems are the less time it will take you and the more money you will make per hour committed.

Benefit #2: You Can Minimize Your Risk

Every facet of real estate investing has risk, including wholesaling. You can waste time on deals that never come to fruition, you can get sued, and you could lose money. Unfortunately, there is no "risk-free" way to invest in real estate, like all investment vehicles. Real estate investing always involves some level of risk; however, you can minimize that risk significantly. Your job as an investor is to always understand those risks and try to minimize them in any way you can.

Wholesaling is the only type of real estate transaction where you are typically lining up your buyer while you are still in contract to purchase the property. In fact, when you learn how to fill out a purchase and sale agreement correctly, you can minimize your risk by including contingency clauses in the contract. You can also minimize your risk by limiting the size of your deposit. Thus, with a relatively small deposit you can control a property worth significantly more for an agreed-upon period of time.

Wholesaling is also less susceptible to local market risk. Of course, while you are in contract the property values could go down, but typically you don't see big swings in the market value of real estate in timelines as short as three to six weeks.

Benefit #3: Having Bad Credit Is Not a Large Limiting Factor

Having bad credit is a limiting factor when it comes to obtaining bank financing for a piece of property. However, an unworthy credit score should by no means deter you from wholesaling. As a wholesaler, having a good credit history can help you, but it is not a necessity. If you have horrible credit, it may cost you a few deals during the course of a year by limiting the number of viable exit strategies you have if you have to actually close on the property. However, if you are focused primarily on selling contracts, it will not be a big factor.

Benefit #4: You Can Utilize Other People's Money

As a wholesaler there are two primary ways you can close a transaction:

1. You can sell your purchase contract, often referred to as *assigning* the contract.
2. You can sell the property shortly after you buy it. This strategy is often referred to as a *double closing*, or a *back-to-back closing*, or a *simultaneous closing*.

When you sell or *assign* the contract, you are not selling the property itself. You are actually selling the purchase contract to another buyer for a profit. In this scenario, discussed in detail in later chapters, the buyer you find actually steps into your shoes and buys the property on the favorable terms you negotiated. The buyer you find will also close on the property using his or her funds. This aspect of wholesaling is perfect for investors who are looking for profitable opportunities with relatively little upfront cash investment. Generally, the only money needed to complete this type transaction is a down payment used to secure the contract with the seller. This technique can also yield very high returns in short time periods.

The second way you can wholesale a property is when you *double close*. In a double-closing situation you will first have to close on the property yourself, using your funds. Of course, the money you use can come from a variety of different sources, including private lenders, hard-money lenders, transactional lenders, and banks, just to name a few.

If you have little money to invest in real estate at this time, private lenders are going to be your best option for the short-term funding needed for wholesale deals that you will be double closing. The great thing about working with private lenders is that many private lenders who understand their money is only being utilized on a short-term basis will be more likely to lend at very high loan-to-value ratios, knowing their money will be returned shortly after closing. Likewise, when you work with private lenders interest rates and points are completely negotiable.

Benefit #5: Time Freedom

Over the past decade of investing in real estate there have been very few days where I rolled out of bed not looking forward to what my day would bring. Real estate investing is not easy; however, I truly believe it is a heck of a lot easier and financially more rewarding than working 40 years of your life for a corporation, the government, or someone else. Working a nine-to-five job swapping time for money is incredibly unfulfilling for many people. After the futility of it finally hits home, many people realize that being your own boss may not be such a bad thing after all.

Having time freedom and total control of your schedule is an amazingly rewarding feeling. I personally feel incredibly blessed to control my schedule because it allows me to spend time with the people I care about most.

Real estate investing, like any profession, can become very involved no matter what facet you specialize in. However, wholesaling requires the least commitment. You are not rehabbing or redeveloping the property and you are not dealing with tenants. So if you are the type of person who loves to travel, or take extended periods of time off, then wholesaling will be right up your alley.

Benefit #6: It Is Challenging, and Never Boring

Obviously, wholesaling can be financially rewarding. However, I believe in order to live a truly fulfilled life you have to be passionate about what you do on a daily basis. I also believe that as humans we seek challenge and through those challenges we discover things about ourselves we never would have discovered had we not pushed ourselves outside of our comfort zone.

One of the reasons I love wholesaling is because it is challenging and no two deals are alike due to the fact that every property and every person involved in the transaction is unique. Thus, you will continually have to think on your feet in order to succeed.

I have also found wholesaling to be extremely exciting, especially considering a large portion of your personal time will be spent hunting, evaluating, negotiating, and closing deals. I have always found chasing deals, or "the hunt," to be one of the most exciting parts of wholesaling and investing in real estate. There is something intrinsically rewarding about finding hidden opportunities that other people have overlooked.

If you like working with different kinds of people, or shopping for bargains, or even chasing the opposite sex, then I truly believe you will draw a great deal of pleasure from wholesaling real estate. It is a feeling that I just can't explain but that you will relate to when you close your first big deal.

Benefit #7: Wholesaling Is a Gateway to Other Real Estate Niches

Wholesaling is also a great way to learn the transactional side of real estate investing. From learning how to find properties outside of traditional channels, to evaluating deals, to learning how to structure contracts, to discounting liens, to learning how to perform double closings, you will learn a great deal about how to navigate through complicated multiparty transactions. When you move into other facets of real estate that have the potential for a larger upside this knowledge will prove to be invaluable.

For example, Steve Hall, who is one of our coaching students from California, started out working with primarily single-family residential properties. With our help, and his determination, he grew a very successful residential real estate investment company. As his knowledge of the business grew with each subsequent transaction he felt comfortable enough to venture into larger commercial real estate investments. On one of Steve's most recent deals he purchased a large hotel in Savannah, Georgia, and is in the middle of renovating and repositioning the property and is poised to make a very substantial profit from the deal. As you can imagine, wholesaling can be a great way to build your knowledge base and confidence and can propel you into even bigger ventures.

CONCLUSION

There are no statistics or proof backing this statement, but I have always had a gut feeling that wholesaling and investing in real estate actually makes you more attractive.

I also believe real estate investors are sexier, better lovers, and generally nicer people than any other type of investor.

In all sincerity, success in real estate is a lot like working out. You can't expect to spend a week in the gym and be fit for life. Likewise, you can't just read one book and expect to be an expert.

Keep accumulating knowledge. The market is mercurial, legislation changes constantly, technology evolves rapidly, and new opportunities present themselves every single day. Commit to spending a few hours each week educating yourself on anything and everything related to investing in real estate.

I highly recommend you also find a mentor, someone with a successful track record, who can help coach and guide you. Your probability for financial success will increase dramatically when you have someone who is looking at your investing efforts from the outside. I believe a coach can see what you sometimes can't and can provide you with strategic advice that will save you tremendous amounts of time, help you avoid costly mistakes, and help you reach your goals in a shorter time frame.

Ultimately, success comes from staying on top of the game. This means knowing your local real estate market backwards and forwards. The next chapter will give you a strategy for doing exactly that.

CHAPTER 2

Getting to Know Your Local Real Estate Market

Be curious always! For knowledge will not acquire you: you must acquire it.

—Sudie Back

During our first year of business, my business partners and I lost quite a few good deals to other investors who had superior knowledge of the market in which we were working. Often, a property would hit the market or the seller would contact us looking for an offer. But we were too slow in our analysis because we didn't know the particular neighborhood or property values, and as a result we ended up losing a lot of those deals. We decided that we needed to gain a better understanding of the local real estate market, neighborhoods within that market, and trends that affected values within that market.

Getting an understanding of the local real estate market will allow you to make better decisions about how you use your time. You will be less likely to waste time evaluating properties that have little or no profit potential. Having a strong knowledge of the market also helps you recognize opportunities quicker. At the same time it will help you avoid costly pitfalls.

THE IMPORTANCE OF GAINING INTIMATE LOCAL MARKET KNOWLEDGE

Before you start marketing to find motivated sellers or making offers on properties it is imperative to study the local real estate market in which you plan on investing. I believe you should research the market you live in, the markets that closely surround you, and the subsections or neighborhoods within those markets. This research will give you a better understanding of the overall market and what trends affect the market.

This initial market research will allow you to make quicker decisions on good deals that present themselves. It is often the difference between getting a good deal and or losing it to a competitor.

It doesn't matter where you invest; there are always opportunities in every local real estate market and in every cycle. Your intimate market knowledge will become a competitive advantage because you will be able to move faster than other people. This market knowledge will also help you to spot opportunities others can't see.

Here are some initial steps you can take to get a better understanding of your local real estate market.

STEP 1: GAIN AN UNDERSTANDING OF LOCAL MARKET METRICS

National real estate statistics dominate the headlines in the media, but local real estate statistics are just as important. If you are seeking to understand a market better and want to identify emerging trends, then there are a few local market statistics you should get to know and track.

Market inventory is an important number to track and watch how it changes over time. Market inventory is the number of houses officially listed for sale at any given time and how long it would take for them to sell at their current pace. This number is usually based on the number of properties currently listed for sale on the Multiple Listing Service. It is important to note that this number does not usually include houses that are for sale by owner as that statistic is extremely difficult to track. Regardless, the market inventory will tell you the current supply of houses that are available for sale.

The rule of thumb is that a balanced market usually has six months' worth of supply. If there is less supply, then it is considered to be a sellers' market. If there is more supply, it is considered to be a buyers' market. In either market there are opportunities for investors. It is less about what the market is doing and more about what you are doing within that market. Sophisticated and knowledgeable investors make money in both up and down markets.

Another key metric to understand is the *average days on market*, which is the median number of days a house is officially listed for sale before it goes to contract. This is an important metric to track when you are negotiating with sellers and agents. It is also important to know because you will always be basing your offers on the profit potential of the deal *if* you were planning on rehabbing or redeveloping the property. The average days on market is an important metric for properly calculating how many months you would have to hold the property if you were to redevelop it. We talk about how to evaluate deals in a later chapter in the book.

One of the most important metrics to know and track in your local market is the *median sale price*. You can often find this data by city, neighborhood, or zip code in your area. The median sale price is the price literally in the middle if you line up all the property sales that quarter from lowest to highest. Generally, this number is tracked by quarter and released by the local Board of Realtors. Websites like Trulia.com also have this data for different zip codes.

The final metric to know and track overtime is the foreclosure rate. This information is often released on a quarterly or monthly basis depending on the area and is calculated by the total number of new foreclosure filings divided by the total number of standing homes in the area. It is important to track this information because when the foreclosure rate increases it can decrease property values months later.

Typically, the most relevant real estate metrics will come from data that is collected by your local Board of Realtors. Usually, the local Board of Realtors aggregates data from local and regional property databases and releases its findings to the public every quarter. I would highly recommend you set up a Google alert for local real estate data and have it sent to your e-mail inbox.

STEP 2: GET TO KNOW PRICE POINTS OF PROPERTIES BY NEIGHBORHOOD

The second step in getting to know your local real estate market is to gain an understanding of median property values of residential properties by neighborhood or subdivision. I suggest you purchase a very large map of your market, put it on your wall, and then make divisions or groupings on the map based on the median price point ranges of homes within neighborhoods or subdivisions.

For example, you may find neighborhoods where the median price point home ranges between $200,000 and $225,000. However, in another neighborhood that borders that neighborhood the median sale price may be much higher or lower. Obviously, there are many different reasons for median price point value swings between neighborhoods. You need to determine what those differences are and where the dividing line exists between neighborhoods. This will also help you locate transitional areas between neighborhoods. This large map will help you gain a better understanding of the market and all the neighborhoods and zip codes that make up that market.

It is important to note that although location is very important, *sometimes* it doesn't really matter where you invest. Opportunities are everywhere, hidden in every market, even in local markets that are typically viewed as very grim. The key here is that you gain an understanding of the unique aspects of your own specific market and use that knowledge to your advantage.

STEP 3: UNDERSTAND ZONING LAWS WITHIN THE MARKET

Pick up a zoning map of the market you plan on investing in and learn what the zoning regulations are for certain neighborhoods within which you are going to be buying. There are many hidden and profitable opportunities to be discovered by gaining an understanding of local zoning ordinances. Understanding zoning laws and how they affect property values will help you discover a lot of development and redevelopment opportunities that you can tie up and then wholesale to other investors.

Let's say you are considering buying a single-family property that is in a commercial area. With proper due diligence you may find that properties are renting for $1 per square foot and office space is renting for $2 per square foot. If you check the zoning, you may find that the property would increase in value if it were converted to office space. Through your knowledge and understanding of your local zoning laws you could make a sizeable profit on a property like this.

Additionally, pay attention anytime a zoning law changes in your local area. Often, affected property owners don't realize the change. Many times, property owners don't understand or investigate the more profitable uses that the new zoning laws permit.

Alternatively, you may choose to pursue these zoning changes yourself on a property you have under contract or tied up with an option to purchase. If you can get elected officials to grant your property a higher and better use, you immediately have increased the potential value of the property. This could be anything from getting an approval to add a second story on a single-family house, to subdividing a lot and selling off a buildable lot, to changing a property's use.

I would strongly advise you to attend a few planning and zoning meetings in your area because you will learn how the zoning process works, meet key players who make decisions within the city, and get insider knowledge on newly proposed developments that are being planned.

STEP 4: STUDY YOUR COMPETITION

As you study the local market you should also start to identify other real estate investors who are frequently purchasing properties in your area. I highly suggest you make a list of these individuals, watch what they do, and reach out to them to build relationships. Work with your competition, because working together will take you so much further than trying to operate your business on an island of secrecy. In fact, your larger competitors will be a great asset to your real estate business and will end up buying a lot of your wholesale deals from you. The more sophisticated they are the less likely they are to waste your time.

Over the years we have sold more wholesale deals to our direct competitors than anyone else. In our slower months we have also bought many wholesale deals from our competitors that we chose to rehab.

There are always ways to work with your competition for mutual benefit. You may find your competitors are only focused on one or two facets of real estate, yet they often identify opportunities outside of those niches. For example, they may not prefer to negotiate short sales on properties, and if you do, then it could be a great way to work together.

STEP 5: IDENTIFY KEY REAL ESTATE PROFESSIONALS IN THE MARKET

It is also important to locate, find, and build relationships with other successful real estate professionals who have a great understanding of the local market. Here is a short list of experienced local professionals you want to identify and build relationships with:

- Realtors
- Hard-money lenders
- Mortgage brokers
- Contractors
- Building department officials
- Building inspectors
- Appraisers
- Title companies/attorneys
- Insurance agents

Each of these professionals can provide you with strategic advice about a property, or a neighborhood, and help you make better decisions when you are making your offers or trying to close a deal. You can leverage their knowledge and years of experience, especially if you have taken the time to develop a solid relationship with them.

SET YOUR FOCUS

After you have completed all five steps you should identify what neighborhoods and types of properties you want to focus on. It will probably be easier for you to focus on residential properties located in middle-income and lower-income neighborhoods while you are getting started. The reason is that you will find a higher percentage of distressed properties in these areas.

Plus, the largest pool of rehabbers or investor buyers will also be looking to buy properties in these areas. It is better to start in a target-rich environment when you're getting started rather than focusing on high-end homes where your pool of buyers will be smaller. This does not mean there aren't deals in nicer areas or other facets of real estate. It is just a good rule-of-thumb for people reading this book who may be new to wholesaling.

CONCLUSION

The biggest reason most wholesale investors fail is that they just don't have a decent understanding of what is going on in their local market. If you don't know what's going on, you can't expect to make informed decisions. Analyzing an entire market is an ongoing process. You've got to be aware of the changes happening within it at all times. If you constantly pay close attention to the market, opportunities will present themselves.

Once you understand your local market, you're prepared to take your business to the next level. In the next chapter, I'll cover some of the basic actions you must take to build a marketing presence and credibility for your wholesaling business.

CHAPTER 3

Establishing Your Marketing Presence

A successful man is one who can lay a firm foundation with the bricks others have thrown at him.

—DAVID BRINKLEY

The most successful real estate investors and wholesalers have one key thing in common: they are also expert marketers. To thrive as a wholesaler, you have to find the best deals. And to find the best deals, you need to know how to market effectively. Without effective marketing, you won't generate any leads. And without any leads, you have no business.

Effective marketers know how to do three things. First, they understand that every business needs to have a *marketing presence*. Second, they know how to *target* people who are motivated to sell. Finally, they know how to get those people to *respond* to their marketing campaigns.

In this chapter, you will gain insight into the key marketing materials you need to establish a marketing presence and credibility for your business so you can jumpstart your wholesaling business.

FOUNDATIONAL MARKETING MATERIALS

There are nine essential marketing tools every real estate wholesaler must have when opening up shop: business cards, seller credibility packets, buyer credibility packets, private money credibility packets, core websites, a Facebook page for your business, an easy-to-remember phone number, a memorable business name, and a logo. These tools will establish identity and credibility for your business and be the foundation on which you build your brand.

Let's take a closer look at the items in your marketing arsenal.

BUSINESS CARDS

The first step is to have a professional-looking business card. A business card is an inexpensive and essential tool that all real estate investors must have. Business cards will let people know you are in business, and can highlight the services you provide as an investor. They can also help to enhance your personal image.

I highly recommend you put your picture on your business card because studies have shown that people are more likely to hold onto a business card that has a photo on it. As a marketer you always want to stand out from the crowd in any way you can.

SELLER CREDIBILITY PACKET

When you meet with a seller, it is essential to build trust and rapport because sellers don't know you, nor do they know much about your business. That's where a seller credibility packet can come in handy. Essentially, it is a multipage marketing brochure about your business and the services that you offer that differentiate you from other investors and real estate professionals. It's something you can present to sellers when you meet with them for the first time. It's also something that sellers can look at after you meet with them.

Many sellers will reject your initial offer or need more time to think about it. So it is essential to provide information about your company that communicates that you are trustworthy and an established professional. It's also additional information the sellers can flip through if they are taking a few days to mull over your offer.

Your seller credibility packet should include your:

- Full contact information (phone number, e-mail, website, and office address).
- Core services your business offers sellers who don't necessarily want to sell through a real estate agent.
- Any additional services your business provides that sellers would be interested in besides just selling their property. These could include relocation services, moving services, credit repair, and anything else that might benefit the seller.
- A description of your business and some basic personal information. Keep this brief. Most people don't care about you or your personal history. They want to know how you can help them and what's in it for them.

- Testimonials from past sellers whose properties you have bought, describing how easy it was to work with you and how professional you were. If you are brand-new in the business, then put some testimonials together from any other real estate professionals you have dealt with or your accountant, attorney, or insurance professional, or even friends.

In all seriousness, whatever you do, make sure the packets are professionally printed and have some great, stock imagery that makes them look really nice. Also make sure you always have a few of them in your car—you never know who you might bump into.

BUYER CREDIBILITY PACKET

On the flipside, you will also meet with a lot of other investor buyers. This is why it is also essential to have a buyer credibility packet.

Like a seller credibility packet, it should include your essential contact information, core services, additional services, business/personal information, and testimonials. The difference is that everything—especially your services—should be *geared toward buyers* instead of sellers.

PRIVATE MONEY CREDIBILITY PACKET

Obviously, raising money for your deals is an essential part of the business and this is why you must have a third packet of information. This credibility packet is geared toward private lenders who may be interested in funding your real estate deals. During the course of your daily interactions, you will meet many people who could be potential private lenders for your deals, and that's why you must have marketing materials that show people the opportunity to potentially earn a high rate of return as a private lender.

A private money credibility packet is something you will give or e-mail to potential lenders when they have expressed interest in private lending.

This packet should include your full contact information, company history, how private lending works, case studies of deals you have completed, your buying philosophy, the terms you offer, and testimonials from other lenders you have worked with in the past. It should also include a very detailed section with answers to at least 10 to 20 of the most frequently asked questions that all new lenders will have.

Many of the real estate investor students we have coached have found that having a private lender credibility packet has helped them answer a lot of people's questions about how the private money lending process works. I have consistently gotten feedback that they have had to spend less time convincing lenders because a lot of their most common questions are answered within the private money credibility packet.

CORE WEBSITE

All successful wholesalers must have a dominant online presence. In fact, the majority of all sellers and buyers who are looking to sell or buy a property start the process by searching for solutions on the Internet.

You need to have a core website for your business that is professional and something you can use to establish credibility, generate leads, and sell/rent your properties.

On your core website you should have the following:

- *Home page tab:* This tab should include an overview of your company and what you do. On the upper right-hand corner of your website, you must have a place where a potential visitor can join your e-mail list. On your home page you should also have full contact information so people can get ahold of you via phone or e-mail.
- *About Us tab:* This is a web page where a visitor can get more detailed information about you, your company, and anybody who works for you.
- *Sellers tab:* When someone clicks on this tab, it sends the visitor to a page that speaks directly to sellers and discusses all the ways you can help sellers by purchasing their property. On this page you should have a web form where sellers can begin the process by giving you some basic information about the property for sale so you can follow up with them.
- *Buyers tab:* This page on your site is geared specifically to buyers who are looking to purchase properties. You should have all your properties for sale on this page, as well as a web form where potential buyers can submit their information so you can follow up with them.
- *Blog tab:* To keep content on your site fresh and to add value to your clients' lives, you should write one article a week that can be posted to your blog. This will help generate leads and is a great way to stay in touch and inform your clients.
- *Properties for Rent tab:* If you have a lot of rental inventory, this is where you can list your properties for rent.

- *Resources tab:* If you have great affiliate relationships with real estate–related products and services, you can list them here. You can also use this page to generate some affiliate income, which can help you expand your business.

FACEBOOK PAGE FOR YOUR BUSINESS

A Facebook page has many potential benefits for your business. While some of these benefits are similar to having a website, like being able to share basic information about your business, a number are unique to Facebook.

Facebook can raise brand awareness with a seller, buyer, or real estate agent checking you out online since once people *like* your page, they will receive updates on their wall where their friends will also see them. The community you build on your Facebook page is an excellent way to build awareness for your business.

Facebook is also good for search engine optimization. The posts you create, links you share, and comments you make on your Facebook page are indexed by the search engines that can bring you new customers. You can use your Facebook page to drive traffic from your Facebook page to your core website and blog. It's a great way to put your business in front of people every day. Your wholesale deals for sale, general status updates, links and videos, and other information appear in the newsfeeds of other people once they like your page.

Over the years we have added thousands of investor-buyers to our e-mail list within our database who originally found us on Facebook. Right now, Facebook is where investors in your area spend a lot of time interacting with others, so you must have a presence there.

EASY-TO-REMEMBER PHONE NUMBER

If you want to really enhance your marketing response rates, get an easy-to-remember phone number, like cab companies do, that you can use in all your marketing campaigns. Your outdoor marketing response rates will be dramatically better when you have a phone number with repeating digits.

To get an easy-to-remember phone number, call your telephone service provider and ask what numbers are available with repeating digits. If you don't like the list of available numbers, then pick up the phone and start calling easy-to-remember numbers and start making offers to the people who own those numbers until you find one.

You will definitely find someone who is willing to sell his or her number for a couple hundred bucks. I have had numerous coaching students find great phone numbers this way.

MEMORABLE BUSINESS NAME

You need a memorable company name and an equally memorable web URL that corresponds to your company name and conveys what your business does. For example, a name like "William Capital Partners" doesn't convey what the business does. However, "Atlanta Property Buyers" would be more strategic, depending on the niche of the business you pursue. The bottom line is your business name should be strategically chosen and mean something to a potential customer who is hearing it for the first time.

LOGO AND BUSINESS COLOR SCHEMES

Having a memorable logo and consistent color schemes will help boost your response rates. There are a number of online services that can create a relatively inexpensive logo. Your logo colors should ideally match the look and style of the colors you use in all your marketing materials. The important point is to be consistent with the colors you choose.

CONCLUSION

Your marketing foundation establishes credibility for your business. That foundation compels other people to take you seriously—especially when you are new to wholesaling real estate. As your marketing presence continues to grow, it will also generate referral leads from other real estate professionals.

Establishing credibility for your business is extremely important because you will often find yourself working with sellers who are distressed. In fact, many will be in pre-foreclosure. But before you can target these motivated sellers, you need to have a solid grasp of the pre-foreclosure process. The next chapter will take you through the nuts-and-bolts of that process.

CHAPTER 4

Understanding the Pre-Foreclosure Process

Opportunity is missed by most people because it is dressed in overalls and looks like work.

—Thomas A. Edison

After the housing bubble burst in 2007, foreclosures became a nationwide epidemic. Everyone knew someone or had heard of someone whose house had been foreclosed on. This presented a very unique opportunity for real estate investors who had a very good understanding of the pre-foreclosure process.

As you look for good deals to wholesale, sellers in pre-foreclosure will inevitably cross your path. But before you can benefit from them, you have to understand how to navigate through the pre-foreclosure process in general and in your state. This knowledge can unlock some of the best opportunities in your market.

This chapter will give you a good understanding of the foreclosure process and show you how you can benefit from foreclosure opportunities while providing an invaluable and ethical service to people who are in desperate need of selling their house.

DEFINITION OF *FORECLOSURE* AND HOW TO LEARN YOUR STATE'S PROCESS

Foreclosure is the specific legal process in which a lender attempts to recover the balance of a loan from a borrower who has stopped making payments to the lender. The lender then initiates the foreclosure process to force the sale of the asset (property) used as the collateral for the loan.

Each state has statutes that govern and guide the foreclosure process. Thus, it's vitally important you understand and know the process in your state. You can find an extensive guide on state-specific processes by going to: http://www.realtytrac.com/real-estate-guides/foreclosure-laws/.

TYPES OF FORECLOSURE

In the United States there are two types of foreclosure actions used to foreclose on real estate mortgage and deed-of-trust loans: judicial foreclosure and nonjudicial foreclosure.

Judicial Foreclosure

A *judicial foreclosure* means the foreclosure must be processed through the state's court system. A public notice of *lis pendens* or "suit pending," is filed with the county or public recorder to notify the general public about the pending lawsuit against the property owner.

Sequential Outline of the Judicial Foreclosure Process

1. The lender or servicer usually sends out three letters to the borrower about the borrower's nonpayment at day 30, 60, and 90.
2. A lawsuit is filed by the lender in the court system and served to the borrower to officially start the pre-foreclosure process.
3. The borrower has to respond to the foreclosure lawsuit before a court hearing date is set. The borrower can raise objections and delay the process.
   a. Example: procedural foreclosure missteps by the lender.
   b. Example: active duty objection.
4. If the borrower doesn't respond within a certain number of days, which varies by state, then the court will grant a default judgment which allows the lender to move forward with foreclosure.
5. The foreclosure case is heard by a judge in the court and either the lawsuit is dismissed or the judge orders the loan to be foreclosed on by setting a foreclosure auction sale date.
6. The public foreclosure sale date is advertised.
7. At the auction the property is sold to the highest bidder, or, if nobody bids, then the foreclosing lender takes the property back. The proceeds from a sale satisfy obligations of the borrower in the following order:
   a. Mortgage holder.
   b. Other lien holders.
   c. Any leftover proceeds go to the former owner of the property.

8. The borrower may exercise statutory redemption rights after the sale if they exist within the state.
9. A certificate of title or sheriff's deed is given to the winning bidder after the state's statutory redemption period is over.

Nonjudicial Foreclosure

A *nonjudicial* foreclosure is also known as a *foreclosure by power of sale*. This method, which is used by many states, such as California, can be exercised if a power-of-sale clause is included in the mortgage or a deed of trust. The main difference in this method of foreclosure is that the sale takes place without supervision of the court and the lender can invoke its right to foreclose by filing a notice of default with the county or public recorder's office.

Sequential Outline of the Nonjudicial Foreclosure Process

1. The lender or servicer usually sends out three letters to the borrower about the borrower's nonpayment at day 30, 60, and 90.
2. The trustee files a notice of default with the county or public recorder's office.
3. A date for the trustee sale is set. The length of time between the filing of the notice of default and the public trustee sale will vary according to the state you live in. Check your state statutes for this timeline.
4. The trustee's sale is advertised to the public.
5. The trustee's sale takes place and the property is auctioned off to the highest bidder or taken back by the lender if the lender does not get outbid.
6. A trustee's deed is provided to the highest bidder after any statutory redemption period expires. This time period will vary by state.

The Strict Foreclosure Process

In a few states, like Connecticut, Maine, and Vermont, there is a pre-foreclosure nuance called the *strict foreclosure process*. Strict foreclosure occurs when the court determines that the value of the property is less than what is owed to the lender.

Once decided, the judge will set a law day, which allows the borrower a specified period of time to pay off the debt required by the court. If the borrower fails to meet this deadline, the mortgage holder automatically gains the title to the property and does not have an obligation to sell it at auction.

Table 4.1 States' Foreclosure Types and Timelines

State	Judicial	Nonjudicial	Comment	Process Period**	Publish Sale***	Redemption Period**	Sale/NTS
Alabama	•	•	Judicial rarely	49–74	21	365	Trustee
Alaska	•	•	Judicial rarely	105	65	365*	Trustee
Arizona	•	•	Judicial rarely	90+	41	30–180*	Trustee
Arkansas	•	•	Both	70	30	365*	Trustee
California	•		Judicial rarely	117	21	365*	Trustee
Colorado	•	•	Judicial rarely	145	60	None	Trustee
Connecticut	•		Judicial only	62	NA	Court decides	Court
Delaware	•		Judicial only	170–210	60–90	None	Sheriff
Florida	•		Judicial only	135	NA	None	Court
Georgia	•	•	Judicial rarely	37	32	None	Trustee
Hawaii	•	•	Both	220	60	None	Trustee
Idaho		•	Trustee sale	150	45	365	Trustee
Illinois	•		Judicial only	300	NA	90	Court
Indiana	•		Judicial only	261	120	None	Sheriff
Iowa		•	Trustee sale voluntary	160	30	20	Sheriff
Kansas	•		Judicial only	130	21	365	Sheriff
Kentucky	•		Judicial only	147	NA	365	Court
Louisiana	•		Judicial only	180	NA	None	Sheriff
Maine	•		Judicial only	240	30	90	Court
Maryland	•		Judicial only	46	30	Court decides	Court
Massachusetts	•		Judicial only	75	41	None	Court
Michigan		•	Nonjudicial only	60	30	30–365	Sheriff
Minnesota	•	•	Nonjudicial mostly	90–100	7	180	Sheriff
Mississippi	•	•	Nonjudicial mostly	90	30	None	Trustee
Missouri	•	•	Nonjudicial mostly	60	10	365	Trustee
Montana	•	•	Trustee sale mostly	150	50	None	Trustee
Nebraska	•		Judicial only	142	NA	None	Sheriff

30

State			Foreclosure Process	Process Period (Days)*	**	Redemption Period	Sale By
Nevada	•	•	Trustee sale mostly	116	80	None	Trustee
New Hampshire		•	Nonjudicial only	59	24	None	Trustee
New Jersey	•	•	Judicial only	270	NA	10	Sheriff
New Mexico	•	•	Judicial only	180	NA	30–270	Court
New York	•	•	Judicial only	445	NA	None	Court
North Carolina	•	•	Nonjudicial mostly	110	25	None	Sheriff
North Dakota		•	Judicial only	150	NA	180–365	Sheriff
Ohio	•	•	Judicial only	217	NA	None	Sheriff
Oklahoma	•	•	Judicial mostly	186	NA	None	Sheriff
Oregon	•	•	Trustee sale mostly	150	30	180	Trustee
Pennsylvania	•	•	Judicial only	270	NA	None	Sheriff
Rhode Island	•	•	Nonjudicial mostly	62	21	None	Trustee
South Carolina	•	•	Judicial only	150	NA	None	Court
South Dakota	•	•	Judicial mostly	150	23	30–365	Sheriff
Tennessee	•	•	Nonjudicial only	40–45	20–25	730	Trustee
Texas		•	Nonjudicial mostly	27	NA	None	Trustee
Utah	•	•	Nonjudicial only	142	NA	Court decides	Trustee
Vermont	•	•	Judicial only	95	NA	180–365	Court
Virginia	•	•	Trustee sale mostly	45	14–28	None	Trustee
Washington	•	•	Trustee sale mostly	135	90	None	Trustee
Washington D.C.	•	•	Trustee sale only	47	18	None	Trustee
West Virginia	•	•	Trustee sale only	60–90	30–60	None	Trustee
Wisconsin	•		Judicial mostly	290	NA	365	Sheriff
Wyoming	•	•	Nonjudicial mostly	60	25	90–365	Sheriff

Source: www.RealtyTrac.com.
*Judicial foreclosures only.
**In Days

BUYING PROPERTIES FROM PEOPLE IN FORECLOSURE

There are a couple of key things you need to know about property owners who are behind on their payments. First, a lot of people will want to explore options for keeping their house before they consider selling their property. You should always be very upfront with the sellers in pre-foreclosure and let them know that if you can find a way to help them save their house, you will.

Also realize that when you start prospecting for pre-foreclosure properties the majority of homeowners you speak to will owe more than the property is actually worth. In these situations you will have to work with the homeowner and negotiate a *short sale* with the bank. A short sale is when the lender agrees to accept less than it is owed on the existing debt as payment in full.

Buying properties in pre-foreclosure presents multiple challenges. Knowing how to deal with them will give you an edge.

- *Lack of good professionals*. This is a big issue. Gain the specialized knowledge and understand the nuances of the process from start to finish, then apply that knowhow to increase your chances of success.
- *Unskilled negotiators*. An investor working with pre-foreclosures needs to be an effective negotiator in order to convince lien holders to take discounted settlements. As a good negotiator, you can purchase properties with room for investor profit.
- *Conflicting interests*. Working with the conflicting interests of agents, attorneys, and creditors, and the needs of the homeowner—combined with a compressed timeline—can be tough. You must be able to pull all the parties and factors together and engineer a solution in order to create an all-around win-win outcome where all parties have their needs met and benefit from the transaction.
- *Late arrivals*. The complexity of these transactions makes it critical to get in front of the homeowner in foreclosure as early in the process as possible. In all my experiences as an investor, the timing—being there first—has been one of the most important factors that can positively affect your success rate.
- *Emotionally charged*. Selling a property in foreclosure is frequently wrapped in a lot of emotions for the homeowner. Understand that, and work to make the homeowner feel comfortable and trust you by being a knowledgeable, no-nonsense solutions provider. Strike the balance of being empathetic without getting caught up in the emotions of the situation.

CONCLUSION

Understanding the pre-foreclosure process is critical when dealing with sellers who are going through this experience. Stay up to date, get an attorney on your team who knows how it works, and familiarize yourself with the rules specific to your state. These things make the difference between success and failure when working with a property owner in pre-foreclosure.

But where do you find those opportunities? The next chapter will equip you with specific techniques designed to home in on pre-foreclosure deals.

Coaching Student Success Story

**FIGURE 4.1 Coaching Students
Linda & Andrew**
Reproduced by permission of Linda Pedersen.

Coaching Students' Names: Linda Pedersen and Andrew Brown
Property Location: Cedar Park, TX
Purchase Price: $105,000
Holding Costs: $3,000
Sale Price: $127,000
Profit: $19,000

(continued)

(continued)

Student Story: Linda Pedersen and Andrew Brown are two coaching students from Texas who were both working full time in the corporate world before getting into real estate. Both were working long hours and had a desire to spend more time with their three children at home. They have completed multiple wholesale and rehab deals and their real estate income has now surpassed their prior income and they couldn't be happier.

　　Deal Summary: Linda and Andrew found this property in Cedar Park, Texas, on a list of properties set to go to auction. They went to the property and knocked on the door and ended up speaking to the owners at length about the property and two days later they had it under contract to purchase at $105,000.

　　Because Linda and Andrew understood the pre-foreclosure process in Texas they were able to act very quickly and were able to stop the foreclosure, pay off the mortgage, and put money in the homeowners' pocket, giving them a fresh start. They also gave the homeowners extra time to move out. Had the home actually gone to auction, none of this would have happened.

FIGURE 4.2　Cedar Park, TX Real Estate Deal
Reproduced by permission of Linda Pedersen.

Initially, they planned on rehabbing the property because there was a tremendous potential upside to the deal. However, after letting a few of our other coaching students in the area know about the deal, they got an offer on the property for $127,000. They ended up double closing on the property and made a profit of $19,000.

Our other coaching students who bought the property from them ended up rehabbing the property and selling it for a nice profit themselves. In the end, Linda and Andrew relied heavily on our coaching advice as we showed them how to pull auction lists, how to accurately assess the after-repair value of the property, and how to network with other coaching students to find buyers.

For more information about our coaching go to: www.FortuneBuildersMastery .com.

CHAPTER 5

Finding Pre-Foreclosure Properties

To know what you know and what you do not know, that is true knowledge.

—CONFUCIUS

The unmatched opportunity that comes with pre-foreclosure properties is too large to even consider passing up. In over a decade of business, pre-foreclosures have been one of the best sources of deals for my partners and myself, and they can be a key part of launching your career as a successful real estate wholesaler.

The previous chapter introduced you to how the pre-foreclosure process works. In this chapter, you are going to build on that knowledge base. What can you expect when you start marketing to property owners going through pre-foreclosure? How can you find the pre-foreclosure list in your area, ideally long before the properties on the list go to auction?

When you know where and how to look, pre-foreclosures can be a big stepping-stone on your path to success as a wholesaler.

FINDING RECENT PRE-FORECLOSURE PROPERTY FILINGS

Many novice investors believe it's difficult to obtain a list of property owners in pre-foreclosure. The reality is it's fairly easy to do. To get a pre-foreclosure list you have two options: (1) you can put the list together manually by going down to your local county government office and searching for and finding the recent *lis pendens* or notice of default filings; or (2) you can buy the list from a pre-foreclosure list provider. I highly recommend going down to the local county government office in person if you are serious about learning about the foreclosure process, since you can take advantage of the clerks' knowledge and gather other lists while you're down there.

Remember, the pre-foreclosure process differs from state to state. When you take a trip down to your local county government office you will be looking for recent *lis pendens* or a notice of default filings. These documents will be recorded, which is the official notice that a property is being foreclosed upon by a lender.

A *lis pendens* is filed in judicial foreclosure actions. The notice of default, on the other hand, is filed in nonjudicial foreclosure actions. In this scenario, the lenders do not file a lawsuit but rather file this document directly on the land records to provide proper notice to the public that the property is in foreclosure and that the lender is intending to sell the property, usually via a private trustee's sale.

Here is an overview of key information you'll be able to identify from these documents:

- Date of the *lis pendens* or NOD
- Names and addresses of the mortgagor (borrower) in default
- Name and addresses of the mortgagee (lender) foreclosing on the loan
- Case or notice default number
- Property address
- Property's legal description or "Schedule A"
- Property's zoning detail
- Property's tax assessment
- Loan amount
- Date the loan was made
- Date last payment was made
- Amount in default (*arrears*)
- Outstanding balance at time of case filing
- Date of auction or trustee's sale

Another reason I recommend physically going to the office and making friends with the clerk is because he or she can be a great source of information, help explain the documents to you, and teach you how to pull the pre-foreclosure list manually. The clerk may also be able to point you to legal publication where foreclosure notices are posted in print. The clerk may even have knowledge of the best local pre-foreclosure list provider from whom you can buy the list each month.

Either way, if you are serious about learning the foreclosure process, don't skip the step of physically going down to the county office and learning how to pull and read these records manually. Don't get frustrated if you talk to someone who is not that helpful the first time you go. Realize the clerk's helpfulness is going to totally depend on whom you speak with, how long the person has been working in the office, and his or her personality type. If you speak to someone who is not helpful, then take a second trip and see if you can find someone who has a good working knowledge of the office.

You can also find pre-foreclosure property filings from the following sources:

- *Newspaper:* In most states, foreclosing lenders are generally required to publish legal foreclosure notices in a locally circulated newspaper. A phone call or a visit to your county clerk's office will put you on the right path to finding the newspaper that has been approved for such notices. You may also be able to find your state's publications by going to this website: http://www.mypublicnotices.com.
- *Online:* In some counties, the quickest and most efficient way to find public records on pending foreclosures is online. To check online, run a quick search for *"your county notice of default or lis pendens records."* You can also call or visit your clerk's office to find out where these are published online.
- *Pre-foreclosure list brokers:* A number of pre-foreclosure list providers and data broker services sell pre-foreclosure data to investors and other real estate professionals. Subscribe to one in your area if there is one available. Their pricing will vary based on where you live, how many records are available each month, and the list broker you use. However, a small monthly or annual subscription investment is *more* than worth it. We have made a lot of money over the years marketing to pre-foreclosure property owners.

 We currently offer some high-quality lists that are very valuable to your real estate investing business. We are also currently working on providing pre-foreclosure lists in certain states. By the time of this publication, you may be able to get a list through us depending on what state you live in. To see what lists are available and in what states, visit this website: www.reiLeadsDemo.com.
- *Marketing to property owners in pre-foreclosure:* There are many different ways to market directly and indirectly to pre-foreclosure property owners. Here are a few ways you can broadly target property owners in pre-foreclosure:
  - Place Craigslist ads targeting property owners in pre-foreclosure.
  - Create targeted pay-per-click campaigns for people searching "Foreclosure Help"–type keywords.
  - Create Facebook ads geared specifically toward property owners in pre-foreclosure.
  - Do outdoor advertising, from bus benches to vehicle signs, to banners, to bandit signs.

- Utilize the Multiple Listing Service to look for pre-foreclosure properties and short sale opportunities.

Over the years we have gotten the best response from doing two specific pre-foreclosure campaigns: direct mail and pre-foreclosure door packets. I'll discuss these strategies further in upcoming chapters.

CONCLUSION

Property owners in pre-foreclosure are some of the most motivated individuals you will work with in this business, and they will provide you with a steady source of good deals. Always gear at least part of your marketing plan toward pre-foreclosures.

Reaching out to pre-foreclosures and other motivated buyers can be done in any number of ways. One of the most effective is through direct mail. In the next chapter, I will show you how to launch a direct mail marketing campaign that builds your brand and rakes in leads.

CHAPTER **6**

Finding Wholesale Deals Utilizing Direct Mail Campaigns

Opinion is the medium between knowledge and ignorance.

—PLATO

Ours is an age of exceptional technology. Money moves at the touch of a button. People on opposite ends of the earth meet and become great friends without ever seeing each other face to face. People camp out in lines that stretch around the block to get their hands on the latest gadget that promises to make their lives faster, more efficient, and more innovative.

And yet, as unbelievable as it sounds, direct mail is still one of the most powerful and proven marketing tools in today's fast-paced world.

There are plenty of reasons why I and many successful investors around the country have been using direct mail for years. First, it's measurable—you can track your responses and easily calculate your *return on investment* (ROI). Second, it's easy to execute, even for novice investors. Third, it's relatively cheap compared to some other forms of marketing.

Over the years I have bought a lot of properties from people who responded to my direct mail campaigns. However, you have to understand the intricacies of direct mail if you want to have long-term success with this marketing medium.

In this chapter you will learn why you should be utilizing direct mail, what lists you should target, how to increase your response rates, and what systems you need to have in place to test, track, and measure the performance of your campaigns. Follow these nine steps to successfully launch your business into direct mail marketing.

STEP 1: FIND THE BEST LIST

Choosing the best direct mail list is an extremely important step. It has been shown that 40 percent of your success from the direct mail marketing campaign will come from those whom you are targeting based on the mailing list you choose. There are several types of targeted lists to choose from.

Pre-Foreclosure Property Owners

In the previous chapter we discussed how to find pre-foreclosure properties either by putting together the list manually at the county recorder's office or by purchasing it from a list provider. Sometimes title companies in your area can also provide you with a pre-foreclosure list. However, the only downside is that the list may be a little old by the time you get it.

The key is to make sure you are getting the list as close to the date of the *lis pendens* or notice of default filing. So always check the date of the filing against the date you actually receive the list.

Out-of-State Landlords

For years we have targeted out-of-state landlords. Out-of-state landlords often don't do the best job of keeping their properties up, especially if they are trying to self-manage the property from afar. These landlords also have less of an emotional attachment to their property, making it easier to do business with them. In addition, a lot of landlords own more than one property, so you might be able to wholesale multiple properties from the same owner.

There are a number of different places where you can get an out-of-state landlord list:

- Directly from a list provider or data broker.
- From the local tax assessor's website. A lot of times you will have to manually put together this list because you can only look up properties individually.
- Some tax assessors' offices sell the complete list of all property owners in the area and will provide it to you in Excel format on a disc. Not all tax assessors' offices do this, but it does not hurt to ask. You can then sort the list and find the landlords with an out-of-state address.

Probates and Inherited Properties

A *probate* is the legal process that settles a deceased person's final debts and formally passes the legal title of their property to the intended heirs. More often than not, the heirs to an estate would much rather sell the property rather than turn the property into a rental. We have found that most probate properties are usually older, dated, and vacant, which makes them great wholesale deals.

Probate records are accessible to the public at the probate court office. In some states this office is known as the *circuit court*, *surrogate's court*, or the *orphans' court*. In general, an estate has been probated in the county where the deceased person lived at the time of his or her death.

When you go down to the probate court most offices will have a computer system where you can look up recent probate court dockets. It is a time-consuming process so make sure when you visit the probate court for the first time you get the clerk to help you. On the positive side, there are very few areas where this list can be bought from a list broker. This means you will have very little competition when you market to a probate list.

Free-and-Clear Landlords

Another list we like to target are landlords who own their properties free and clear, meaning there is no debt recorded against the property. Generally speaking, most landlords who own properties free and clear have owned those properties for a number of years. Many times these properties have a lot of deferred maintenance and were bought for significantly less than what they are presently worth. The best way to obtain this list is through a list provider.

Expired Listings

An expired listing is when a listing agreement between a seller and a licensed real estate agent expires. For whatever reason, the house was on the market, but the listing agent wasn't able to get the property sold.

To obtain expired listings, you will need to work with an agent who has access to the Multiple Listing Service (MLS). The agent can send you a current list of expired listings in Excel format that you will then market, too.

Delinquent Property Tax List

A delinquent property tax list is a list of property owners who have failed to pay their property taxes. A lot of times these properties will also have deferred maintenance, which makes them great wholesale deals if the seller is motivated. You can locate delinquent property tax lists by asking the clerk down at your local tax assessor's office. Some areas will sell this list to you for a small fee and others will show you how you can put the list together manually.

STEP 2: DECIDE HOW MANY TIMES YOU WILL MAIL THE PROSPECT

When it comes to direct mail marketing, consistency is one of the keys to success. Many sellers won't contact you until you have mailed them at least three or four times. Thus, you will want to create a multistep campaign, and it's important to set your budget accordingly. For example, let's say you had a $1,000 budget and each direct mail piece cost you $1 to mail. You will generally be better off mailing 250 people four times than you would mailing 1,000 people only one time.

Once you have determined your budget and the size of the list make sure you are committed to following through with all the mailings. I see a lot of real estate investors give up after sending out one direct mail campaign because they didn't get the response they wanted from the first piece. Remember, the response rate improves each time you send a subsequent direct mail piece when you are dealing with sellers.

STEP 3: CREATE A SPREADSHEET TO TRACK YOUR MAILINGS

Tracking your mail campaigns is vitally important to maximizing your return on investment. You want to know what campaigns went out to what lists, what mail pieces got returned so you can take those people off future mailings, and what letters have not yet been sent out.

It's also important to track the cost involved with each step of the campaign by individual letter or postcard. You'll also want to track your responses from each campaign, as you will need to know what works and what doesn't. That way, you are better able to tweak pieces that aren't performing up to your expectations. The easiest way to track all of this is in an Excel spreadsheet or a Google spreadsheet.

STEP 4: DETERMINE WHAT TYPES OF DIRECT MAIL PIECES YOU WILL USE

People ask me all the time, which gets a better response rate: a postcard or a letter? It depends on many different factors, such as who else is mailing the list and what types of direct mail pieces they are using. More specifically, it depends on what the direct mail piece actually says and whether it is compelling to the owner of the property. The important thing is to vary what type of direct mail piece you send out if you are mailing multistep campaigns. There are four types of direct mail that I would suggest you use.

Short Letters

Short letters work well because you are not really saying much about who you are, what you do, or why you are interested in buying the property. Many times you will find that sellers call you just because they are curious. Figure 6.1 is an example of a short letter.

Long Letters

Sending a seller a longer letter gives you more of an opportunity to tell the seller how you can help him. The key is to give the seller as many reasons as you can think of to pick up the phone and call you to discuss selling his home. Spell out as many benefits of working with you as you can within the letter.

Dear (Seller Last Name,)

I am looking to purchase a home in the (Neighborhood Name) in the next thirty days or so. The other day I drove by your house and it looked perfect! I have cash and would be willing to make you an all cash offer in the next 72 hours.

Give me a call right away at 555.555.5555.

Sincerely,

(Your Name)

FIGURE 6.1   Short Letter

Yellow Letters

A *yellow letter* is a letter that looks handwritten and is printed on yellow lined notebook paper. The reason this type of marketing piece will generally get you a higher response rate is because it looks like you took the time to sit down and personally write the homeowner a handwritten letter. The piece is meant to look like it is coming from a friend and will definitely draw the attention of the property owner. We have found these letters to be very effective.

Postcards

Always include at least one postcard in your multistep direct mail campaigns. Postcards are obviously a lot cheaper to mail than letters. When you send a postcard you can almost guarantee that the seller will read it because he doesn't have to open a letter. The disadvantage is that it usually doesn't look as personal and because you only have so much room to compel the seller to call you. Once again, you should definitely create curiosity with the piece to generate a higher response rate.

Here are some tips on how to make your postcard more appealing:

- Give the mailing a personalized feel by hand-writing the prospect's name and address on the postcard.
- Use unique and interesting stamps. This will generate some curiosity from the prospect and the longer she looks at your postcard, the better the chance your message will have to reach her.

Lumpy Mail

An old direct mail trick that can definitely boost your response rates is using lumpy mail. Lumpy mail is just like it sounds: lumpy. Inside your letter you include something like a piece of candy so that your letter is not flat. People will be curious about what's inside so they will definitely open your letter. This will also get your letter and your message to stand out.

STEP 5: CRAFT A COMPELLING MESSAGE

Now let's talk about the actual format of your letter and your copy. The text you will want to include in your letters or postcards should persuade the homeowners to take action and contact you about selling their property. Your prospects should feel as though you understand their personal situation and are speaking directly to them with the copy that you write. Let's break down the different parts of a mail piece.

Have a Compelling Headline

Your headline is the single most important thing at the top of your letter or on the front of your postcard (or envelope). When you look at your direct mail piece, ask yourself, "What catches someone's attention?" If your answer isn't the headline, you might want to make some tweaks. Your headline should be clear, catchy, and bold.

Headline Examples

- "Sell Your Property in 10 Days . . . Guaranteed!"
- "How You Can Sell Your House without Paying a Dime in Commissions"
- "I Can Make You an All-Cash Offer on Your House in 48 Hours or Less!"

Be Empathetic

Distressed sellers often feel very alone and many are extremely frustrated with their situation. Thus, it is important to be empathetic to their situation. Let them know they are not alone and you genuinely want to help them by providing them with a solution to their problem.

Empathetic Statement Examples

- "Every year, hundreds of thousands of people face foreclosure and unfortunately a lot of people just don't know what options are available to them."
- "If you have ever had tenant problems, you are not alone."
- "We have helped hundreds of homeowners like yourself see a better future."

Offer Benefits

Never assume the sellers know the benefits of what you're offering—you need to break it down for them. How are you going to help them? What is your *unique selling proposition* (USP) that sets you apart from the rest?

Your offer should be *tailored* to getting the reader to take action today. Think of reasons why prospective sellers would choose to do business with you and craft the benefits around those reasons.

Offer Benefit Examples

- *No agent commission:* "You can save a lot of money selling the house yourself!"
- *No repairs needed:* "We buy properties in as-is condition and you don't have to put a single dollar into your property."
- *No stress:* "We make selling your house as easy as possible. We can make you an *all-cash* offer on your house in 48 hours. There is absolutely no obligation and all your information is kept completely confidential."

Call-to-Action

Your direct mail piece must have a very clear *call-to-action* letting the prospect know exactly how to get ahold of you. Ideally, you incorporate a sense of urgency in your copy so the prospect picks up the phone or visits your website right away.

Call-to-Action Example

- "Call me directly at 555–555–5555 as I am looking to purchase a property in your neighborhood in the next 30 days. You have everything to gain and nothing to lose!"

Your Contact Information

This seems like a no-brainer, but many people forget to add this, or they have it in small print. Your contact info should be prominent, right below your call-to-action.

A Guarantee or Bold Promise

Companies are afraid of guarantees, but people *love* them. A guarantee helps your prospects feel comfortable and builds trust that you really want to do right by them.

Guarantee Example:

- "Get a guaranteed *all-cash* offer in 48 hours or less!"

STEP 6: CHOOSE POSTAGE

There are many postage options available when distributing your direct mail campaigns. Here are some available options to you:

- *First-class mail:* It's quicker than most other large mailing options, and comes with an advantage: Mail sent with bad addresses is returned to you so you can update your database.

- *Presorted first-class mail:* This option offers you a price savings over first-class mail. To receive the discount, you must have 500 or more pieces in the mailing and sort (or group) the mail by zip code.
- *Standard mail:* Formerly known as "bulk" mail, standard mail costs less than first-class mail, but it doesn't provide address-correction services. A minimum of 200 pieces or 50 pounds of mail is required.

If you're doing a large mailing (and plan on doing them on a regular basis), you might want to consider investing in a postage meter. You'll be able to post large batches of mail in no time at all. If you're doing a smaller quantity, save yourself a trip to the post office by using an online postage service, which allows you to print postage stamps directly from your computer. Most investors prefer to outsource this task to a company with the knowledge and equipment needed to fulfill their direct mail campaigns at the lowest postage possible.

STEP 7: SET UP YOUR INBOUND SYSTEM

Before you even think about sending out a direct mail piece, you must decide how you're going to handle responses. Are you going to take phone calls in your office? Are you going to use a call center? Or are you going to send your prospects to your website to submit information to you? Here are a few ways:

- *Call center:* Create a script and intake form so phone reps can answer calls for you 24/7 and e-mail/fax you the lead sheets for your review.
- *Google Voice:* A virtual service that can be redirected to a third-party number (your cell or office). The system also records and transcribes the voicemails and e-mails them to you for review at your convenience.
- *Website squeeze page:* If you're going to be driving your leads to a website, you need to make sure you have a web form on the site where your prospects can fill out and submit their information.

STEP 8: FULFILL YOUR CAMPAIGNS

Many investors choose to start by fulfilling their campaigns themselves, especially in the beginning. Obviously, fulfilling your list in-house will be cheaper than outsourcing it, but it will also be very time consuming. I would suggest you do a few campaigns yourself only if money is really tight. In many cases, you are going to be a lot better off outsourcing your direct mail campaigns and hiring someone on an hourly basis to do the work for you; or you can set up a relationship with a direct mail fulfillment company. Your time is better used educating yourself, evaluating deals, making offers, and building your business.

STEP 9: NOTE RESPONSE RATES

Be careful not have unrealistic expectations with your response rate. Large direct mail marketers are consistently trying to beat a 1 percent response rate. Also, when sending bulk mail, expect to receive 8–10 percent of your mailings returned for bad addresses.

Remember, consistency is the key. You will likely get responses from your first mailing; however, most people won't respond until the third or fourth time you have mailed them. Sometimes, sellers will look at your mail piece for months or longer before they pick up the phone to call you. In that case, *you* want to be the one still mailing to these folks when they finally become motivated; and they will remember you because your message has been in front of them many different times. Remember, timing is everything and circumstances change over time.

Helpful Tips for Your Mailings

- Live postage (any direct mail piece with a normal stamp and not metered postage) and handwritten notes will increase your response rate.
- Use colored or odd-sized envelopes for even better results.
- Stamps sometimes outperform metered mail.
- Personalize your piece with the seller's name and the property address that you are interested in.
- Colored stationery/mail piece/letterhead (see-through window).

CONCLUSION

Direct mail campaigns have brought us countless properties over the years. But it isn't the only way we find wholesale bargains. In the next chapter, I'll give you a foolproof system for finding deals using the Multiple Listing Service.

Coaching Student Success Story

FIGURE 6.2   Coaching Student: Quincy Smith
Reproduced by permission of Quincy Smith.

Coaching Student's Name: Quincy Smith
Property Location: Midlothian, VA
Purchase Price: $60,000
Transaction Costs: $3,000
Sale Price: $75,000
Profit: $12,000

Deal Summary: Shortly after joining the coaching program Quincy found this deal from a motivated seller who responded to one of his probate direct mail campaigns. (He used one of our exact direct mail letters that we give to our coaching students.) The property was located in a nice neighborhood, but had significant fire damage. The seller, an attorney, owed $58,000 after the insurance claim, so Quincy agreed to purchase the property for $60,000. The seller was not in a big hurry to sell the property so Quincy structured a 90-day escrow so he could find a buyer.

(continued)

(continued)

FIGURE 6.3   Real Estate Deal in Midlothian, VA
Reproduced by permission of Quincy Smith.

Quincy then began marketing the property to his buyers' list and by placing listings on Craigslist and Backpage. He found a buyer less than two weeks later with whom he went to contract to sell the property for $75,000.

Quincy also built a pretty good buyers' list because he kept marketing the property even though it was under contract all the way up until closing.

Quincy ended up making a profit of $12,000 on the deal when he sold the property. Since this deal he has now sold 10 properties and currently has three under construction. Quincy is also a captain in the Army and is now at a point where he's able to choose whether to continue with a career in the Army or devote himself full-time to his real estate investing business. He's also providing a better lifestyle for his family and their future.

For more information on applying for coaching go to www.FortuneBuilders Mastery.com.

CHAPTER 7

Finding Deals on the Multiple Listing Service

Mistakes are the portals of discovery.

—James Joyce

My real estate business looks very different today than it did 10 years ago when it was only my business partner and I living and working out of my condo in New Haven, Connecticut. Fast forward a decade, and our business has mushroomed into a very large company with a team of people working for us. Many things have changed; however, some things have not. The *Multiple Listing Service* (MLS) is one source of quality wholesale deals that has remained very consistent for the past 10 years.

The MLS is a suite of services and software that enables real estate brokers and agents representing sellers under a listing contract to widely share information about properties for sale. Almost every successful student we coach has bought deals right out of the MLS and has made it part of his or her marketing and acquisition process.

As great as the MLS is, however, there's a catch. The majority of the properties listed on the multiple listing service are owned by sellers who aren't motivated to sell their property at a discount to an investor.

Don't let that discourage you. There are plenty of deals on the MLS. The key to finding them is to have a system for sifting and sorting through MLS postings in place. If you learn and implement what I am about to teach you, you will set yourself up for a stream of continuous deals. This chapter presents a system for farming your local Multiple Listing Service. I call it the *MLS offer system*.

THE MLS OFFER SYSTEM

The MLS offer system is a process we use every day to farm through new and existing listings in our area to find bargain properties that we can then sell to bargain hunters.

Within this MLS offer system, you will be researching newly listed properties to try to find pre-foreclosure properties, REO properties that are owned by banks, and distressed properties that need work. I have divided this system into seven steps to make it easy to understand and follow.

Step 1: Filter and Find Potentially Distressed Properties

First, you need to learn how to properly run effective searches within the MLS. To get access to the MLS you have to become a licensed real estate agent or broker, which I highly recommend. In some areas a real estate agent can have an unlicensed assistant, so check with the local Board of Realtors and what its policy is with giving access to unlicensed assistants. If you choose not to get licensed, then you will have to have a real estate agent set the search criteria up for you and assist you in doing a lot of the research, which can be cumbersome. If you have to consistently rely on real estate agents to get you information about properties, it will slow you down and you will lose out on a significant percentage of deals.

Next, research all newly listed MLS properties every day. Speed is an advantage. The MLS can be highly competitive, so you definitely want to be the first one to know about a good deal when it hits the market.

In the areas we target, between 50 and 150 properties typically hit the market every day. Of those properties, only 10–15 percent will have what we consider true investor potential and will need to be researched further.

We identify these types of properties by searching through the remarks that agents make about the properties, such as *fixer*, *must sell*, *cracked slab*, *TLC*, *contractor*, *gut*, *work*, *motivated*, *quick close*, *cash*, and *handy*. We also search for special financing key terms like *203k*, *Homepath*, *Homestep*, *Fannie Mae*, and *renovation financing*.

Finally, we look through the pictures for properties that show signs of distress. If the property needs a lot of work, the owner usually doesn't have the desire or the finances available to fix the property up to maximize the value.

Once you have filtered down your search to a handful of properties that have a higher probability of being deals, you can start contacting the listing agents to gather more information.

As the final part of this step, keep a record of all the properties and agents that you reach out to. This is important because a lot of your success will be determined by how good of a follow-up system you have. We create new property records in our database for every new property we are going to contact the agent about. We also create a new contact record within our database every time we speak to a new agent about a property. This is invaluable because you will be calling certain agents multiple times over the course of a year and you want to remember whom you spoke with and which property you spoke with them about.

Step 2: Reach Out to the Listing Agent

The next step involves contacting the listing agent to gather more information about the property, the seller, and the overall situation. First, you want to know how much activity the property has had and whether the seller is open to offers from investors. If you find that the agent is focused on finding retail buyers, then the property will become a lower priority. If the agent is open to working with investors, then you will want to investigate the property further.

Remember, the agent works for the seller, but there are a lot of benefits you can offer the agent that a lot of retail buyers can't. Here are a few things you might be able to offer to get the agent excited to be working with you:

- Both sides of the commission if you are not working with a buyer's agent
- A cash offer
- An offer with very few contingencies
- A quick close or a closing that is ideal to the seller
- Future leads on unlisted properties if you are marketing in any other way
- Access to your team and the network you have built
- Help with the short-sale negotiation in a pre-foreclosure situation where the seller owes more than the property is worth
- The possibility of repeat business over the course of a year

Again, keep a record of all the properties and agents that you reach out to.

Step 3: Run Comparables

Once you have spoken with the agent and it sounds like she believes the seller would be interested in working with an investor, then you should run *comparables* on the property to assess its market value. Comparable sales are property sales used for purposes of comparison in the real estate appraisal process. Ideally, they are relatively similar to the subject property, open market transactions, and with a time of sale close to the date of value. We discuss how to do this in more detail in later chapters.

Step 4: Walk Through the Property

Once you have run your comparables you should go visit the property to examine its condition and to make an estimate of the repairs the property needs. In order to do this you will have to set up a time to view the property when you speak with the agent over the phone.

Step 5: Drive by the Comparables to Determine the After-Repair Value

After you walk through the subject property, drive by the comparable sales in the area in order to determine the after-repair value or how much the property would sell for once it's fixed up.

Step 6: Make an Offer

Once a property makes it through the all of these steps you should be ready to make an offer. If you have discussed having the listing agent represent you, then you will have her write the offer up. If you aren't, then you will write the offer up and e-mail it to the agent and then follow up with a phone call.

If the offer is accepted, then you will start the closing process. If the offer is countered, then you may want to negotiate. If the seller just isn't motivated enough, then you will want to follow up and resubmit an offer 30, 60, and 90 days later, if the property is still on the market.

Step 7: Follow Up

In about 30 percent of the deals we get using this MLS offer system the seller was originally not interested. However, over time some sellers become more motivated if they can't get a higher offer or if they have a buyer that falls out of contract. It is critical to have a really good follow-up system so you can aggressively follow up on properties you have made offers on. Use your database to set up a strong follow-up system.

OUTSOURCE STEPS WITHIN THE SYSTEM

When you start out you will be the one who is doing all the work. However, after you wholesale a few deals I suggest hiring an assistant or a virtual assistant you can train to help you work this system. If you develop systems and work *on* your business, rather than *in* your business, you will quickly replace yourself in each role.

CONCLUSION

Using the MLS effectively means having solid systems in place. My system took years to create, refine, and test. In fact, during the first three years of our business, I focused two days a week purely on building systems and looking for ways to create step-by-step business processes. I made this activity a priority, so I could eventually leverage my time effectively and build a business that did not depend on me. These are the systems we now pass on to our coaching students so they do not have to reinvent the wheel, easily shaving years off their learning curves.

The MLS isn't the only source available to you when it comes to scouring the Internet for wholesale deals. In the next chapter, we'll look at how you can use Craigslist to find more properties at optimal prices.

CHAPTER 8

Finding Deals Utilizing Craigslist

The Internet is like a giant jellyfish. You can't step on it. You can't go around it. You've got to get through it.

—John Evans

Before computers ruled our lives, a lot of real estate investors perused the classified sections of local newspapers, hunting for deals. Each morning, they sat down at their kitchen tables, red pen in hand, and peeled through page after page of tiny black print, circling potential properties that caught their eye. Then they picked up the phone, punched in the numbers scrawled next to their notes, and called up the owners or listing agents to get more information.

Today, just like most everything else, the classified world has gone digital. There are search bars and hyperlinks. You don't pay to print, but simply click to refresh.

Craigslist is one of many online classified websites. On Craigslist, sellers create free classified advertisements to promote their properties for sale. Craigslist has become the top classified advertisement website, attracting millions of users each month. And it can be a powerful tool for your wholesaling business if you use it consistently and correctly.

SEARCHING FOR PROPERTIES UNDER THE "REAL ESTATE FOR SALE" SECTION

When you click on Craigslist's "Real Estate for Sale" section, you will find that you can sort the listings "by broker" or "by owner." Almost all the properties listed under "by broker" will also be listed on the Multiple Listing Service.

Instead, we focus on the properties that are listed "by owner." Plenty of properties for sale are not good deals. Occasionally, though, you will find a property that is a gem. Check it daily and only call on properties that look like they need work and would be fixer-uppers.

SEARCHING FOR PROPERTIES BY KEYWORD

Another way to search Craigslist for properties is by *keyword*. The exact search terms you use are very important. You want to look for signs of motivation in the sellers' advertising copy. Instead of using generic terms like "houses for sale" that focus just on the actual property you will want to use search terms that are geared toward locating motivated sellers.

Here are a few common search terms that can be useful for locating homeowners who need to sell their property:

- "Motivated seller"
- "Rent to own"
- "Take over payments"
- "Will finance," or "Owner will finance"
- "Seller will carry second," or "Seller second available"
- "Lease option"
- "Owner desperate"
- "Homeowner must sell"
- "All offers welcome," or "Considering all offers"
- "Will sell on terms," or "Terms available"
- "House must go"
- "OBO," or "Or best offer"
- "Flexible seller," or "Flexible terms"
- "Creative financing OK"

CONTACTING LANDLORDS WHO ARE RENTING PROPERTIES

Another great way to find potentially motivated sellers is to contact property owners who have created rental listings and posted them on Craigslist. On Craigslist there is an entire section for apartment and property rental listings under "Apts/Housing for Rent."

When you sort through these listings, you will find the majority of them will have been created by either a property management company or a real estate agent. You want to focus only on the properties being rented by the owner directly.

The majority of landlords don't respond to inquiries about selling their properties—however, a few will. Typically, when landlords do respond to our e-mail it is either out of curiosity to see what we would offer or because they are motivated and frustrated with being a landlord.

CONTACTING PEOPLE HAVING ESTATE SALES

Another great way to find potentially motivated sellers is to contact people having estate sales who are selling furniture, appliances, or other household items on Craigslist. Many people holding estate sales are clearing out the possessions of the house before they put it up for sale or are in the process of selling the house.

Reply via e-mail to the individuals who created the "estate sale" listings to see if they might be interested in selling the property as well.

CREATING ADVERTISEMENTS THAT GET PEOPLE TO CONTACT YOU

In addition to searching through other people's advertisements, you can also create advertisements to get people who are interested in selling to contact you on Craigslist. Start by placing them in the "Real Estate for Sale" section. A lot of agents and owners who are selling properties will check these listings before they create a new listing for their property.

CREATING A COMPELLING AD TITLE/HEADLINE

When your create ads on Craigslist you must have an attention-grabbing headline. The body of your advertisement can be incredibly good, but if the prospect doesn't even click on the ad, then it is worthless. Browse the site and look at what advertisements catch your eye. Then use those same elements when you are creating your headline.

If you're posting a lot of ads, be sure to use a different title for each ad—even if it is merely a different symbol or special character at the beginning or end of the title. Make sure each ad is unique and slightly different from the others you posted. Never repeat ad titles or descriptions or else you'll run the risk of your ads being *ghosted* by Craigslist, meaning that the ad will appear to have been posted, but will not show up in the listings.

Ghosting is when your ads seem to have been posted successfully; however, Craigslist actually hides the ads from visitors. These ads are not searchable, nor do they appear on the site. Ultimately, Craigslist is trying to avoid marketers spamming their site, so if they see something they don't like about your post, they shut it down before it even goes live. You might think your ad was posted, but it may not be.

The easiest way to get ghosted by Craigslist is to post a ton of ads in the first few days of setting up your account, and also having similarities in ad titles and descriptions. Be steady and post ads every day, and just stay consistent. It's a marathon, not a sprint.

USING SYMBOLS TO MAKE YOUR TITLE/HEADLINE STAND OUT

One way to make your headline stand out on Craigslist is to use symbols and special characters in the headline that draw attention. Using stars, hearts, and other symbols in the ad headline/title will improve the open-rate.

Here are examples of some symbols on codes. You'd put these codes before or after your title text:

▶▶	&#9654
◆◆	&#9830
▲	&#9650

For instance, using one of these example codes, you post this Craigslist title and code:

▶ ▶ Sell Your House in 7 Days or Less ▶ ▶
   That title will show up on Craigslist like this:

▶▶Sell Your House in 7 Days or Less ▶▶

WHAT THE BODY OF YOUR ADVERTISEMENT SHOULD COMMUNICATE

Once you have compelled a seller to click on your advertisement, your goal is to get the seller to either call you, visit your website, or reply to your advertisement via e-mail.

Remember, you will have a wide variety of different types of sellers looking at your advertisement so your copy should include a variety of compelling reasons why someone should call you or click on the link to visit your website. Here are a few example bullets you might want to include:

- "Pay *no* commissions to sell your house."
- "We buy properties in all conditions and in all areas."

- "We can make you an offer on your property in 48 hours or less and there is absolutely no obligation."
- "We can close on a timeline that fits your schedule."
- "We can help even if you are behind on payments or owe more than your house is worth."

Always include a link to your website or ideally a squeeze (lead capture) page. A *squeeze page* is a website set up specifically to convert traffic into leads. On the website prospects can enter some basic information about themselves, including their name, phone number, e-mail, and property address.

Image Ads versus Text Ads

Another way to get your advertisement to stand out on Craigslist is to include an image within the body of your advertisement. I've tested both, and when you have a good image it will always increase your response rates. Some people sort advertisements on Craigslist and only look at ones that include an image. Thus, even if you plan on using mostly text in your ad you should still include a small image.

Make sure you use unique images in your ads; if you repeatedly use the same image over and over again, you will get ghosted rather quickly. A great solution is to make copies of images you're using in your ads and rename each one so Craigslist will think these are all unique images.

Reposting Your Ads

Your ad has to be older than 48 hours and you have to delete the original ad first, before reposting the ad.

But because it's important to keep your ads on top, there's a second option: you can also create multiple versions of your ad with modified headlines, location tag, and content. If your ad is different, it won't be ghosted.

Boost Your Account's Reputation

Craigslist will let you bend the rules on posting multiple similar ads if you are posting from an account that has paid Craigslist for something (i.e., $25 for a job posting). It's not ghosting-proof, but it helps.

Getting Flagged

If you post Craigslist ads often, you should prepare to be *flagged*—and that's okay. According to Craigslist terms of use, users may flag postings they believe to be in violation of Craigslist guidelines by clicking on one of the flagging links at the upper-right corner of each posting.

Keep in mind that Craigslist itself doesn't do the flagging; most often, it's other competitors flagging your ads, attempting to get yours taken down and have their ads shown instead. Just be consistent, keep posting your ads, and eventually they will get tired and give up.

Although it's completely normal to get flagged, excessive flagging can cause your account to be put on hold or deleted. Proceed with caution when making multiple posts, and if you find that you're getting tons of flags for "over-posting," cut down a bit or just spread out the amount of time between your posts.

CONCLUSION

As with most advertising, test and track your Craigslist results by including *tracking codes* within your ads in combination with your own website analytics. Through these tracking methods, you can determine the effectiveness of your ad. The data you collect over time will reveal when activity is the highest and when you're likely to get the most views, thereby maximizing your effectiveness on Craigslist.

Direct mail, the Multiple Listing Service, and Craigslist are three of the top ways we cull the market for great wholesale deals. But they're far from the only ways to find great properties. In the next chapter, I'll run you through several other options for digging up good investments.

CHAPTER 9

Other Killer Ways to Find Profitable Real Estate Deals

Success always occurs in private, and failure in full view.

—Anonymous

The most successful wholesalers are always the most successful marketers. And the most successful marketers have three key things going for them: they're creative, they're consistent, and they're constantly tracking results.

If you're creative, your marketing stands out from the crowd, and people who are ready to sell their property right now decide to contact you. If you're consistent, you capture people's "mind share" and compel them to pick up the phone or visit your website when they are ready to sell their house down the road. And if you're constantly tracking your results, then you know what campaigns are working, which ones aren't, and how to invest your marketing dollars to maximize your return.

When you have these three things—creativity, consistency, and tracking of results—you can combine them with just about any strategy to make that strategy effective in finding great wholesale deals.

In this chapter, you'll get the rundown on other marketing campaigns that have proven effective for me, my business partners, and our coaching students over the years. All of them embody creativity, consistency, and tracking. The important thing is not to be dependent on only one source of leads. Diversity is key to making consistent money from wholesaling properties.

PURCHASING INTERNET LEADS

Buying real estate investing Internet leads can be a very attractive and profitable way to give your wholesaling business a boost and hit the ground running. You could turn on this lead source today and you'll probably have leads waiting for you in your inbox within the next few days.

The majority of homeowners looking to sell their home start gathering information online to assist them in going through the home selling process. In response, many companies have formulated businesses around capturing these seller leads and reselling the information to real estate investors and professionals in the market from which the lead came. These companies are essentially wholesalers of real estate leads they generate with SEO (search engine optimization) and pay-per-click campaigns. Their business model is relatively simple. They target certain keywords that motivated sellers would be searching and advertise on the search results. When sellers click on their ads, it takes them to a landing page that encourages the sellers to fill out a web form to sell their house. The company then sells that lead to an investor in the area—generally for a set fee per lead. Many times, it costs the lead generation company a considerable amount of money to generate the lead—they can cost anywhere from $25 to $100 each. However, this cost is small compared to the return you can generate on the properties you end up buying.

An easy way to find which companies are selling leads to investors in your area is to search terms that motivated sellers would be utilizing and click on their ads. Usually, on their landing pages there will be a link about how to buy leads from the company.

Terms You May Want to Search
- "Sell house fast"
- "Stop foreclosure"
- "Sell house without a realtor"
- "We buy houses cash"

QUESTIONS TO ASK ABOUT PURCHASING INTERNET LEADS

Finding a reliable source for real estate investing Internet leads is the most important step. When you get ready to purchase leads from an online lead provider, make sure that you ask these questions:

- How many leads do you generate on average per month?
- What is the cost of those leads?
- How much information is given to you?

- What types of leads are being sold in your area and what types of real estate professionals are buying them?
- Do you have to buy a minimum number of leads per month?
- Do you have exclusivity? (Does the lead provider sell that lead multiple times to other investors, agents, or any other real estate professionals?) Ask the lead provider if they put a cap on how many times the lead is sold.

The more you are willing to pay, the more exclusive the leads should be and the higher your closing ratios should be, ultimately resulting in higher profits.

FACEBOOK

When looking for a simple and effective marketing technique, look no further than Facebook. If you haven't utilized Facebook, then you are missing out on a major opportunity to expand your business's web presence.

You won't necessarily get a lot of motivated sellers contacting you directly from your Facebook profile or business page, but you will find that other investors and real estate agents will reach out to you if you consistently post on Facebook. Having the ability to put your business in front of people every day in a social way is a great way to generate referral leads.

Also, be aware that when people type your name into a search engine, typically your Facebook profile or business page is one of the first items to show up. When creating your personal page, make sure that it is professional, and yet have a bit of charisma as well.

The key is to integrate social media into your preexisting marketing campaigns. For instance, if you're blogging, automatically post each new article on Facebook as well. You should also include links to your social media pages at the bottom of your e-mail and the bottom of your website. You never know who may contact you with information on your next big deal.

FACEBOOK ADS

You can also market for motivated sellers by using Facebook ads. Also known as *pay-per-click advertising*, a great benefit of these ads is that you only pay for the ads when someone clicks on them.

- *Location:* Through Facebook's pay-per-click ads, you can be location specific, meaning you can choose who views your ads. For example, you can target homeowners within 5, 10, 25, or any other number of miles of your area.
- *Demographics:* Facebook pay-per-click ads are demographically specific so you can formulate ads that target only certain age groups.
- *Interest:* As a marketer on Facebook, you can choose to show your ad only to people who are interested in a certain topic. Many people are not aware of this, but Facebook actually uses "likes" and "friend" relationships to assist their marketers in targeting specific users.

OTHER REAL ESTATE PROFESSIONALS AND INVESTORS

As a wholesaler, there are several people that you should be constantly networking with and marketing your business to because they can be great sources of referral leads. Keep in mind that each person you come in contact with while doing business becomes a potential referral source for deals.

- *Other investors:* There are a lot of investors who are just getting started who will inevitably refer you deals that they can't put together. You might also consider doing a joint venture with them on a wholesale deal.
- *Real estate agents and brokers:* Obviously, agents and brokers can be a great source of referral leads. When people think of selling their home, agents are usually the people they think of first, so having relationships with good agents is a vital part of being a successful wholesaler.
- *Mortgage brokers:* A lot of sellers reach out to mortgage brokers either because they are trying to refinance their property if they are behind on payments or because they are in the process of getting qualified to buy another house before they sell their existing home. This is a great opportunity for you to get a lead on a house that has not yet been listed.
- *Attorneys:* There are many different types of attorneys who could refer you motivated seller leads because they work with people in situations such as pre-foreclosure, bankruptcy, probate, landlords evicting tenants, and divorce.

There are many other individuals who also can be great referral sources, such as title agents, insurance agents, hard-money lenders, building department officials, contractors, and, of course, family and friends. We have gotten deals from every one of these individuals over the years.

DOOR HANGERS

Door hangers are an unconventional form of marketing that you can use to get your message in front of a large group of homeowners in an area of town where you frequently purchase properties. Door hangers are almost impossible for a homeowner to miss because they are literally hanging from the door handle. They also stand out because there are no envelopes to open, nor do they get lost in the sea of junk mail. Make sure the copy you use on the door hanger would appeal to a wide variety of people who might be motivated and interested in selling their properties relatively quickly.

BUS BENCH ADVERTISING

Believe it or not, advertising with bus benches works and can potentially be a very viable source of leads in areas in which you consistently buy properties. Typically located along busy streets, bus-stop benches provide excellent exposure and capture the attention of vehicle drivers, pedestrians, and public transit commuters in passing. You will be highly visible to the thousands of people who are driving by these road signs.

Realize when you use bus benches you only have a few seconds to make an impression, so make sure your message is simple, clear, and easy to read—something like "We Buy Houses Cash" with your phone number.

The key is to have an easy-to-remember phone number that one doesn't have to write down. Any phone number with repeating digits is going to be much easier to remember for a prospect driving by your bus bench.

You also want to be very strategic in your placements of this type of advertising. We've found that placing advertising on benches located near stoplights and intersections in major metropolitan cities works the best, since drivers and passengers will be actively looking for entertainment while they await the green light.

Most bus bench advertising companies will have a minimum number of benches they will sell, so don't expect to just buy one bench. The rates vary based on how many benches you are going to advertise on and the number of months you lock in on the advertising contract.

BANNERS

Large banners are a great alternative or addition to the large yard signs or bandit signs that you put in front of the house. Every time we buy a property to rehab we hang a large 4′ × 12′ banner from the front of the house. This can be a great form of marketing, especially if you have a lot of projects under construction. These banners come in several different sizes.

The great thing about purchasing properties from banner leads is that they tend to be in the same neighborhood as the projects you are currently working on. You might also consider paying residential or commercial property owners in the area who have buildings with a lot of street traffic a small monthly fee to hang your banner off the side of their building.

VEHICLE WRAPS

You drive around from property to property, so why not promote your brand at the same time? Vehicles that are wrapped with large graphics that cover your entire vehicle or a portion of your vehicle are very effective. You are basically turning your vehicle into a roving billboard that will draw a lot of attention.

In wrapping a vehicle you should keep the design simple and clear since your ad will be on the move. The message should also include your company name, phone number, and a simple message such as "We Buy Houses."

Vehicle wraps draw a lot of attention as they are driven around town. But you can also park the vehicle in a highly visible spot when you are not driving it. The best places to park your vehicle are at busy intersections in areas where people do a lot of shopping.

If you rehab a lot of properties using the same contractors, then you might even talk them into putting up some advertising for you on their vehicles that can help you generate more leads and therefore more projects for them. You can even put a special phone number on their vehicles if you want to track the leads back to them versus your vehicles.

We have had great success with wrapping company vehicles over the years. We started with just vinyl letters on one of our work vans. We then purchased a 16-foot box truck for $4,000 and wrapped it because we found a great spot next to a highway that had thousands of cars driving by every day. We then convinced a few of our contractors to let us put signs on their vans. Believe me, you will get phone calls.

CAR MAGNETS

Large car magnets that stick to your car doors are an alternative to wrapping your entire vehicle. Car magnets are relatively inexpensive (less than $200). They won't generate nearly the same number of calls because they are smaller, but they definitely work, and you also have the option of moving them from vehicle to vehicle.

BILLBOARDS

Most electronic media (mobile ads, TV commercials, etc.) can be either skipped or averted by a simple change of the channel, while billboards remain practically unavoidable. Especially while sitting in bumper-to-bumper traffic, an effective billboard can truly grab your attention. Billboards don't move—therefore, your message is conveyed to the same person driving to work or the store, every day at around the same time. Remember, repetition is the key to marketing.

There are many investors who don't receive a very good response from their billboard advertising because they include too much information on them, which prevents individuals from reading all the content.

The cost of traffic billboard advertising depends on the location, size, and how many billboards you lease. Although they work great, the traffic billboards on the interstate are much more expensive. It may be best to start with billboards located in the lower-end areas; the cost is fairly reasonable and they typically provide the best return.

- *Bulletins* are the largest, most high-impact type of billboard used in outdoor advertising. They are located primarily on highways and offer great visibility due to their size (standard size is 14′ × 48′) and creative, customized advertising.

  There are two types of bulletins: *permanent* and *rotary*. Permanent bulletins stay in one place for the duration of the contract. Rotary bulletins are moved to a new location periodically (mostly in two-month cycles).
- *Thirty-sheet posters* are the next-largest-size billboard, ranging from 9′7 × 21′7 to 10′5 × 22′8. They are located mainly in commercial and industrial areas on primary and secondary roads. The main viewing audience is people in vehicles, as well as commuter traffic, residents, and pedestrians. They are generally sold in monthly contracts.
- *Eight-sheet posters* are a bit smaller than the 30-sheet posters and are called *junior posters* by some companies. They are located primarily in urban neighborhoods and on secondary roads. Generally, they are positioned just above eye level as a freestanding unit or possibly on the side of a building. Similar to 30-sheet posters, 8-sheet posters are purchased in monthly units.

TELEVISION ADVERTISING

Over 99 percent of households in the United States own a television set, which makes this a very attractive advertising medium for real estate investors looking to take their business to the next level. Advertising on television can be very powerful and many investors have doubled and tripled the number of leads they receive on a daily basis simply by implementing a successful TV campaign. Sellers like to deal with an established, credible, and professional company and being on TV helps to establish this credibility.

Unfortunately, many investors consider TV advertising to be a marketing medium only used by large companies with unlimited advertising budgets and not something accessible to the average real estate investor. However, with the growth of regional and cable TV in many markets the cost of advertising has gone down significantly because of increased competition for advertising dollars. This is good news for small companies and real estate investors who now can afford to implement quite a significant television campaign to achieve their goals. However, TV advertising is for more experienced investors only, or at least ones with enough capital to run the campaign correctly.

The cost of a television campaign can easily overwhelm new investors who have not built up a significant reserve of capital behind them to keep it running on a regular basis for at least few months. An effective campaign on the low side will initially require a $10,000–$15,000 commitment. Successful campaigns will then require at least $4,000 a month on an ongoing basis to really maximize the number of incoming leads and brand your company or message within the community.

A television campaign will generate a lot of leads in a very short period of time. If you are not prepared to handle these leads with the proper phone system, prescreen them quickly, and organize the data efficiently, then many of your dollars spent on television will be wasted.

CONCLUSION

Every wholesaler needs at least three or four successful marketing campaigns running at once. That way, if one campaign stops working, your whole business doesn't grind to a halt. Track and evaluate your marketing campaigns every month to improve on your response rate and increase your effectiveness. And always be consistent. Repetition of a message is what keeps the phone ringing.

Once you've tracked down your deals, you need to know what to do with them. The next chapter is an overview of how to value real estate.

CHAPTER **10**

Overview of How to Value Real Estate

In order to succeed, your desire for success should be greater than your fear of failure.

—Bill Cosby

You may have heard horror stories about someone who lost a ton of money trying to flip a piece of real estate. Generally, it's because the investor overpaid for the property because he underestimated the cost of repairs or miscalculated what the property would be worth once it was fixed up. Either way, this is never a predicament you want to experience and why the next few chapters are so important.

Correctly appraising the after-repair value of a property is one of the most important skill sets required of you as a wholesaler. Over the next few chapters, you will learn the time-tested process I have been using for years for determining the value of a property, as well as how to avoid the mistake of overpaying. You'll also learn how to build a business process around this skill set to help you evaluate and appraise several properties at once.

There are three common approaches appraisers use when valuing a property: the *cost* approach, the *income* approach, and the *sales comparison* approach.

THE COST APPROACH

The cost approach is generally used for one-of-a-kind, special-use properties, and where market data is extremely scarce. The cost approach gives you a purely cost-based perspective on the market. The cost approach, simply, is an estimate of the replacement value of a property's components—the land and the improvements on the land. Rather than valuing the property as a whole, this approach adds up the separate values for both the land and the improvements. This approach in essence says a buyer would never pay more for a property than the cost of a *comparable* site and building.

THE INCOME APPROACH

The income approach is typically used to value income-producing properties, commercial properties, businesses, and residential properties greater than 5+ units. It is based on the premise of anticipation of future benefits. More specifically, value is related to two things: the market rent or income the property will produce, and the resale value of the property.

THE SALES COMPARISON APPROACH

As an investor who is looking to wholesale residential properties, the majority of the time you will be using the sales comparison approach to determine a property's value. The reason is because this approach is the most indicative of what the true *market value* of the property is, especially if there are plenty of similar sales in close proximity to the subject property.

When you use the sales comparison approach to determine the value of the property you will be itemizing out different elements of the subject property and comparing those elements to other like-type properties that have recently sold within a close proximity to the property, known as *comparable sales*. You will then make adjustments to the value of the subject property based on the differences between elements. There are seven categories of comparison for appraising residential properties:

1. The type of property rights conveyed
2. Financing utilized to purchase the property
3. Terms and conditions of the sale
4. Market conditions in the local area
5. Location components of the property
6. Physical characteristics of the property
7. Economic characteristics

I will specifically discuss the sales comparison approach in the next few chapters. What you will learn is very similar to the approach most appraisers take when valuing a residential property. From my experience in buying and selling hundreds of properties, I did find it necessary to slightly adapt the formal process appraisers take to accommodate a few more property adjustment components.

A WORD OF CAUTION

One thing to be aware of is that property appraisals can be very subjective, especially if the subject property is truly distinctive, either because the property has been individually designed and custom built or because the lot offers special features.

We once sold a property on which the bank required our buyer to get two appraisals. The two appraisals came in $25,000 apart. Both appraisers were very experienced. This is why I believe appraising properties is partly art and partly science.

No matter how experienced of an investor you are, at the end of the day you are still estimating the after-repair value of the property. You will never be able to discover the true value of the property until the property is rehabbed and put back on the market to be resold, and a buyer is found.

Investors who have had multiple appraisals done on the same property within a short time frame of each other understand that the value of the property is always subjective to the person who is performing the appraisal, what information they are accessing, and what comparables they choose to use in their appraisal. It is not uncommon to have two appraisals done by licensed appraisers that yield values that are vastly apart.

ALWAYS DETERMINE THE HIGHEST AND BEST USE OF THE PROPERTY

In the next three chapters I will be walking you through the three-step system I use to evaluate deals in order to determine the after-repair value of the property. This system assumes you will always be looking for the highest and best use of the property. The highest and best use of a property is assumed to be the most profitable legally and physically permitted use of the property. The highest and best use will be determined by an analysis of the zoning laws, the market, the community, the neighborhood, the site, and the improvements. Since the focus of this book is on residential wholesaling, the majority of the time you can assume the highest and best use of the property is going to be a remodeled residential residence.

However, that being said, you will occasionally run across residential properties that are in areas that are zoned commercial, so you will want to also do an after-repair-value analysis of both a residential property and a commercial property. Likewise, you may run across residential properties with large lots that could be subdivided or possibly even rezoned. Thus, you will also want to look at the possibility of another higher and possibly more valuable use of the property in these scenarios.

YOUR GOAL AS A WHOLESALER WHEN MAKING OFFERS

As a wholesaler you have to put the property under contract at a value significantly below the current "as-is" market value of the property, thus creating enough of a margin to generate your profit. The majority of the time you will be selling the contract or selling the property to another investor who also will be looking to earn a profit by rehabbing and reselling the property. These investor-buyers or "rehabbers" will be creating their profit by increasing the value of the property by fixing it up and ultimately putting the property back on the market to sell.

As a wholesaler your value is in finding and negotiating a great deal that would in turn be attractive to other investor-buyers. Of course, any sophisticated wholesaler knows that great real estate deals don't last very long so you not only have to know the technical steps of how to appraise the value of a property accurately, but you also have to be able to do it quickly. This is why having a process and a system for making and tracking your offers is so vital to your long-term success.

CONCLUSION

Valuing real estate accurately is a major cornerstone of success for any wholesaler. In the next three chapters, I break down our process for gathering information from sellers and agents, how we research properties from our desk, and how to calculate the after-repair value of the property when you visit it.

As I go through and describe each one of these three distinct stages I will discuss the intricate details of the research tools we use to perform our due-diligence on properties, the software we use to manage all of the offers we make, and the system we use to track and follow up on all the offers we make. These tools, software, and business processes are what make up our three-step deal evaluation system. This is essential to you as a wholesaler because it will allow you to look at and make offers on more properties on a weekly basis. It will save you a tremendous amount of time, make you more efficient, and ultimately allow you to make more money.

In the next chapter we discuss the first stage of my three-step deal evaluation system and how to gather the information you need to properly appraise the value of the property.

CHAPTER 11

Deal Evaluation System Stage 1

Gathering Information

Success is not final, failure is not fatal: it is the courage to continue that counts.

—Winston Churchill

In my first couple of years as a real estate investor, I wasted an enormous amount of time evaluating properties that weren't deals because I didn't have an efficient process for separating the good ones from the bad ones. I didn't have an effective process to weed out properties that had little or no potential early in the process.

As a wholesaler, you are going to make from 15 to 25 offers on properties before you get one deal under contract. That means you don't have time to waste on properties that don't have the potential of being a deal. The reason you want to divide this process into stages is that you don't want to go through the entire due-diligence process and perform a full after-repair value appraisal on a property when the deal isn't good or the seller isn't motivated.

In the next few chapters I am going to walk you through the three stages of our *deal evaluation system*. I have used this system for the past decade to gather information on a property, perform the necessary due diligence, and properly appraise the after-repair value of the property as efficiently as possible. Best of all, this process ensures that when I put a property under contract it's at a discount.

We'll start with the first stage of the deal evaluation process: gathering information.

VITAL INFORMATION TO GATHER IN STAGE 1

In this first stage of the deal evaluation system you need to gather critical information about the property and the seller's situation. You will get this information from either the seller, agent, or a third party if the deal was referred to you. Here you will find critical information you have to gather broken down into categories.

Seller's Contact Information

This is important information to gather for obvious reasons. If the seller has contacted you directly and is highly motivated, it is even more important. Sellers in financial distress often hide from their problems, so the more information you have about how to get in contact with them the better.

- Property owner's name(s)
- Property owner's phone number(s)
- Property owner's e-mail address(es)
- Property owner's fax number(s)
- Contact person for owner (if there is one)

Realtor's Contact Information

If you are working with real estate agents, they often prefer you work through them as opposed to speaking with the seller directly.

- Real estate agent's name(s)
- Real estate agent's phone number(s)
- Real estate agent's e-mail address(es)
- Real estate agent's fax number(s)

General Property Information

This information is very important to collect because these property parameters are what you will use to pull your comparables. If the seller, agent, or anyone else gives you this information, you should always verify the information by checking it against the property card online and at the property itself.

- Property address
- Type of property—single family, duplex, commercial, etc.

- Style of house if a single family
- Square footage of property
- Bedrooms
- Bathrooms
- Lot size
- Garage
- Does the property have a view or is it located in a special area?
- What amenities does the property have?
- Does the property have any special features?
- What subdivision is the property located in?
- What school district is the property located in?

Current Status of an Owner-Occupied Property

If the seller is currently living in the property, he or she tends to have a stronger emotional attachment to it. Sellers' personal attachment to the property will be even greater if they have lived there a long time and raised a family in the property. If the seller still lives in the property, I also know that I will have to arrange buyer showings around the seller's schedule.

- Does the seller currently live in the property?
- How long has the seller lived in the property?
- When is the seller planning on moving out?

Current Status of a Vacant Property

It is always easier to wholesale a vacant property because you will be able to show the property more easily without disrupting the owner or a tenant who might be living there. The seller usually has less of an attachment to a property that was a rental or that she has moved out of. This could also be a sign of distress depending on the seller's situation.

- How long has the property been vacant?
- Who was living in the property before it was vacated?
- When is the last time the seller has been inside the property?

Current Status of a Rental Property

If the property is currently rented, then you want to gather information about all the tenants, their rents, and their leases. If the property is a multiunit property with a lot of tenants, then you want to gather this information for every single unit. Obviously, if tenants occupy the property and have lengthy leases, this is something your buyer will inherit with the property.

- How many tenants live in the property/unit?
- What is the current rent for the property/unit?
- Is there a security deposit for the property/unit?
- How long have the tenants lived in the property/unit?
- How long is the current tenant's lease for the property/unit?
- Are the tenants part of any Section 8 program or other government subsidized program?
- If they are Section 8, what portion of the rent is Section 8 covering?

Listing Information

Whenever you are analyzing a property you have to find out whether the property is listed with a real estate agent. We buy listed properties all the time and it is something that you need to be aware of because you will often be communicating and negotiating through the agent as opposed to working with the seller directly. Either way, this is the information you want to gather:

- Is the property currently listed with a real estate agent?
- Was the property recently listed with a real estate agent?
- How long has the property been listed?
- What price is the property listed at?
- Has the price on the listing been dropped?
- Have there been any offers on the property?
- What price did the offer(s) come in at?
- Why did the seller not accept the offer(s)?
- Who is the listing agent?
- What is the listing agent's contact information?
- When does the listing expire?

Property Condition and Repairs Needed

It is very important to get a feel for the current condition of a property you are analyzing before you decide whether this deal is worth looking at in person. If the property is listed, there will be a few pictures of the property online or on the listing sheet the agent e-mailed you. If there aren't many pictures of the property, or if the seller has contacted you directly, then you want to ask the seller or agent questions about the condition over the phone. Usually, the best wholesale deals need work. You will very rarely find sellers who are motivated who have properties in pristine condition.

- What repairs does the property need?
- Has the property been updated in any way in the past few years?
- What would you estimate the repair cost to be if this property were to be updated or remodeled?

The Seller's Motivation

It is vitally important to find out if the seller of the property you are analyzing is motivated. You won't get a good deal on a property unless you are working with a motivated seller. Thus, a lot of the properties can be eliminated at this stage of analysis if you find out the seller isn't motivated. When I am working with sellers directly I can usually find out the following information by asking good questions. (It is a little more difficult when you are working through agents because they won't always reveal this information.)

- What is the seller's reason for wanting to sell at this time?
- How quickly is the seller looking to sell the property?
- What is the ideal closing date for the seller?
- What is the seller going to do if the property does not sell?

Current Debt against the Property

Any time you are investigating a deal you need to know if the seller has any equity. Obviously, if there is little or no equity and the seller is current on his mortgage, there won't be much you can do with this deal. If the seller has little or no equity and is behind on his payments to the lender, then the only way to create equity is to negotiate a short sale with the bank.

- What does the seller currently owe in total against the property?
- Does that include all liens and mortgages?
- Is the seller current on his payments?
- If the seller is behind on payments, how many months behind?

Terms of the Underlying Loan(s)

This information is easier to obtain when you are working directly with the seller. The reason you want this information is that you may decide to make the seller an offer "subject to" the existing mortgage. When you buy a property subject to the existing financing, you leave the existing financing in place when you take title to the property—the loan remains in the seller's name, even though the title is under our name as buyers. It is important to note this is not the same as assuming the mortgage, where the loan is transferred to the buyer's name. You are not going to change the name of the borrower or sign for the debt when we buy a property subject to the existing mortgage. If the seller has multiple loans, you need the following information for all loans:

- What is the seller's monthly payment on the loan?
- Does that payment include taxes and insurance?
- What is the interest rate for the loan?
- Is that interest rate fixed or adjustable?
- When was the loan originated?
- Is there a prepayment penalty on the loan?
- Who is the lender?

The Seller's Bottom-Line Price

This is critical information you need to know for obvious reasons. The key is to try to figure out what the seller's bottom line is before you make an offer. If I am working with a seller directly, I can usually get him to tell me what his bottom line is. If I am working with an agent, it is more difficult, because the agent usually won't reveal this because she is protecting her client or because she doesn't know the seller's bottom line.

- What is the bottom-line price the seller will take for the property?
- Is that price flexible?
- If you made the seller a cash offer, could he do any better than that?
- How was the seller's price established?

RECOMMENDED TOOLS TO GATHER AND TRACK INFORMATION

All real estate investors need to have tools, systems, checklists, and processes for tracking information within their businesses. Below I will discuss a few of these tools.

Seller Lead Sheet: Script to Gather Information

If a seller calls you from one of your marketing campaigns, it is very important to build as much trust and rapport with the seller as you can during the initial conversation.

I use a script of questions called a *seller lead sheet* that I fill out when taking a lead from sellers. I have found that having a set process helps me get the information I need from the seller while at the same time allowing me to build trust with the seller. To get a copy of the seller lead sheet I use, visit www.TheWholesalingBible.com and you can download it for free.

It typically takes me about 15 minutes to gather all the information listed earlier from the seller on the initial phone call. As I gather the information about the property and the seller's situation I make initial judgments about the potential of the deal based on the information the seller gives me.

While I am speaking with the seller, I always check out the seller's property by entering the address on Zillow.com. Zillow.com is a property-data-aggregation website with *comparables*. On the site it gives you an automated estimate of the property's value, called a *zestimate*. The zestimate isn't highly accurate because it is an automated valuation, but it gives you a ballpark idea of the property's value based on data aggregated from properties sold within the neighborhood.

Zillow helps me judge if there's any equity or upside to this deal by comparing the property's zestimate with the seller's asking price. Essentially, I am trying to quickly discern whether the seller is looking for retail or is willing to sell at a discounted price.

For example, Zillow might estimate that the house is worth $250,000. If the owner is seeking $250,000 to $350,000, he or she most likely is not a motivated seller. That gives me an idea of how much time to I am going spend with the seller (not much!) and how to handle the lead. But if the seller is asking for a price that is far below the zestimate, then I will schedule an appointment to look at the property right over the phone.

You should know your market area well enough so that when a seller calls you about a property, you have a fair idea of the price of properties in that area. Your intimate market knowledge will give you a competitive advantage, because you can act with a sense of urgency when you come across a really good deal. If someone sounds extremely motivated over the phone, always set an appointment to look at the property. If you run comparables and later find out it isn't a good deal, you can always cancel the appointment.

CRM/Database: To Track All Your Leads and Information

I highly recommend having an online CRM (Client Relationship Management)/database like we use so you can track all of your leads, deals you're analyzing, properties you're making offers on, and properties you have under contract. Likewise, you should use a CRM/database to manage all of your contacts. Having a CRM/database makes managing your real estate business so much easier because all of your critical information is in one place that can be accessed from anywhere with an Internet connection.

The CRM/database we use allows us to create a new property/seller contact record, and all the critical information we gathered in this stage of the deal evaluation system gets transferred into the database. I also scan and save the seller lead sheet and any other documents or contracts to the property/seller contact record. This makes it so much easier for me to analyze multiple deals and offers that I have out at any given time. To see a demo of the system we use, go to www.reiToolDemo.com.

CONCLUSION

Take your time with this stage of the deal evaluation system. Make sure that you ask all the right questions. Otherwise, you'll find yourself spending a lot of time analyzing deals that don't have potential, or worse, making offers on properties that could put you in a very bad financial position.

Thus, you have to get comfortable asking a lot of questions even if the other party is resistant to giving you information. Remember, in any negotiation the person with the most information is the one who usually prospers. That's why it is so important to know what information you are gathering so you can perform your due diligence as well as accurately appraising the after-repair value of the property.

In the next chapter, I'll take you through Stage 2 of the deal evaluation system: starting the appraisal and due-diligence process from your desk.

CHAPTER 12

Deal Evaluation System Stage 2

The Desktop Evaluation

I have failed over and over again in my life and that is why I succeed.

—Michael Jordan

Stage 1 of the deal evaluation system lets you know if you're fishing in the right lake. By the end of Stage 2 of the deal evaluation system—the desktop evaluation—you'll be able to tell whether the fish at the end of your line is a keeper, or if you're better off throwing it back.

In the second stage of the system, you begin to appraise the after-repair value of your potential property, and you start the due-diligence process. You eliminate a lot of leads at this stage, and that saves you time in the long run.

On the other hand, if a property survives this stage of the process, it has the potential to be a serious deal. Follow these nine steps to complete Stage 2 of the deal evaluation process.

STEP 1: CONFIRM THE PROPERTY DETAILS BY REVIEWING THE PROPERTY CARD

Before you start researching comparable sales of like-type properties you must confirm the information the seller, agent, or third party gave you about the property by pulling a property card. Property cards are the city's records of information about a property associated with a single deed. That deed typically represents ownership of a parcel of land and all of its improvements. Typically, property cards include some or all of the following information:

- Transaction sale price history of the property
- Assessed values

- Ownership history
- Land use, zoning approvals, and construction permits
- Land line valuations (acreage, lot dimensions, etc.)
- Building valuations (square footage, year built, replacement cost, etc.)
- Construction details (bedrooms, baths, style, heating/cooling, etc.)
- Building sketches
- Extra features, outbuildings, and subarea dimensions

In most states, but not all, you can access property cards online. The first thing you should do is call the local tax assessor's office or the county property appraiser's office and ask them if the public can access property cards and information online. If you have access to the Multiple Listing Service in your area, you should also check to see if your system includes tax assessor data. A lot of local MLS systems do have tax assessor data that you can use to verify information as well.

If you live in a nondisclosure state like Indiana, Kansas, Mississippi, New Mexico, Utah, or Wyoming, you won't necessarily have access to the sale price of properties on a property card. In these states only the principals and any real estate licensees involved in the transaction will know the sale price. If you live in one of these states, you will have to get sales data from a private company that maintains real property ownership records for your county or from the local Multiple Listing Service.

If there is a big discrepancy between what the agent, or seller, has told you and what you see on the property card, you should flag it and make sure you investigate the discrepancy further. For example, I have had many sellers grossly overestimate the square footage of their property because they either didn't know the square footage or included extra square footage from a finished basement.

STEP 2: PULL THE LISTING SHEET IF THE PROPERTY IS LISTED WITH AN AGENT

If you are analyzing a property that is currently listed by a real estate agent, then you definitely want to have a copy of the property listing sheet. Listing sheets give you important property information entered into the Multiple Listing Service by the agent who has the listing agreement with the seller. Listing sheets can also be printed up with all the interior and exterior pictures the agent had taken of the property.

The MLS listing sheet will provide you much greater detail about a property in comparison to what you will find online from real estate websites like Zillow or Trulia.

The MLS has more information because agents are required to input very detailed information and pictures of the properties they list.

If you have access to the Multiple Listing Service, you should also pull any old listing sheets about the property if the property was on the market at any time in the past. I have had sellers who must have had amnesia—they forget to tell me that their property had recently been listed and pulled off the market.

STEP 3: UNDERSTAND WHAT YOU ARE TRYING TO DETERMINE WITH THE SALES COMPARISON APPROACH

As an investor the majority of the time when you are evaluating one- to four-unit properties you will be using the sales comparison approach to determine the property's after-repair value. The sales comparison approach, also referred to as the *market approach*, is a methodized process of directly comparing the subject property you are evaluating to other properties that have recently sold.

The *as-is market value* is the most probable price the property would sell for in an open and competitive market and is what most appraisers will calculate when performing an appraisal on a traditional sale. This value assumes that both the buyer and seller are motivated, that the property has had a reasonable amount of exposure and time on the market, and that all parties to the transaction are well informed. Real estate investors often refer to the as-is value of a property as its current market value before making any repairs to the property.

However, to analyze the potential of a wholesale deal you will actually be calculating the *after-repair value* of the property. The after-repair value is the price you predict the property would sell for once the property is remodeled and in pristine condition and then put back on the market and resold.

The as-is and after-repair values can be very similar numbers if the property doesn't need a lot of work and is already in very good condition. Obviously, if the property needs a complete renovation, these two numbers are going to be much further apart.

STEP 4: FIND THE BEST COMPARABLES USING THE MULTIPLE LISTING SERVICE

Technically, when you use the sales comparison approach to determine value you will be looking for three or four recent like-type comparable sales. These sales should be considered like-type in that they have similar features and are within close proximity to the subject property. I recommend looking at like-type properties that have not yet sold and are either actively being marketed or under deposit.

Obviously, your determination of value is going to be based primarily on the sold comparables. However, properties that are active and under deposit give you a good sense of how much inventory is available and what direction the market might be heading.

To be considered a recent sale the properties you will be comparing should have sold within the last six months and ideally within the last three months. The acceptability of the sale from a time standpoint will depend on the number of sales that have taken place and the volatility of the marketplace. In a slow-moving market or a rural market you may have to look for comparable sales within the last year. If this is the case, you may have to make a slight adjustment to the price of the subject property you are analyzing, depending on which way the market is moving.

I typically begin my search in a very restrictive manner to see if I can find comparables that are very similar to the subject property. If I can't find enough comparables, then I start adjusting my search criteria until I find the number I need. Generally, my initial search criteria for similar properties are as follows:

Types of Comparables

- Sold, deposit, and active

Type of Property

- Same as the subject property

Sale Date

- Within the last six months

Radius Search

- Less than a half-mile radius from the subject property
- Must be in the same city
- Ideally in the same neighborhood, subdivision, and school district

Square Footage Range

- 80–120 percent of the square footage of the subject property

Bedrooms and Bathrooms

• Same as the subject property

I manipulate my search criteria as necessary. If I don't have enough comparables, which is usually the case, I will expand the number of bedrooms and bathrooms to include a wider range. If I still don't have enough comparables, I will drop the bedrooms and bathrooms altogether. If I still don't have enough comparables, then I will do the following in this order:

• Expand the square footage to 70–130 percent.
• Expand the radius to three-quarters of a mile.
• Expand the radius to one mile.
• Expand the sale date to go back nine months.

I will keep expanding my search criteria until I find three or four good after-repair-value comparable sales that are in really good condition.

At this point I will have my sold comparables and a few properties that are active and under deposit. I will then print all of the comparables I have pulled along with a map of the comparables. Most MLSs will allow you to run a report with a map of all the comparables you have selected. I will then save a PDF version of the map and the comparables within my database so that I always have a record of what I used to make my evaluation.

STEP 5: LOOK FOR OFF-MARKET COMPARABLES

Ideally, when you pull comparables you want to use the Multiple Listing Service in conjunction with any website that gives you access to local tax data. When the owner of a property sells the property without using an agent, the record of the sale may not show up when you are searching the MLS.

This is why you should also use a website or service that also has access to comparable sales from the tax assessor's record. All property sales will be part of tax assessor data records. For example, Zillow.com aggregates tax assessor data and you may occasionally find comparable sales that did not show up in your original MLS search. We are not talking about a lot of properties, because the majority of properties sold in an area will have an agent involved on one or both sides of the transaction. However, there may be one or two good comparables you find that will help you in your after-repair-value financial evaluation.

STEP 6: ANALYZE THE SOLD COMPARABLES TO DETERMINE WHETHER THE PROPERTY IS WORTH VISITING

At this point I generally have enough information to determine whether this lead has the potential of being a good deal. I will flip through the comparable sales and put together a rough estimate of what the after-repair value of the subject property would be.

Steps to Take When Working Directly with the Seller and It Doesn't Look Like a Good Deal

If I know the seller isn't motivated and the property doesn't have a significantly higher after-repair value compared to the price the seller is looking for, then I generally call the seller back and make a very low verbal offer over the phone. I do this even though I know the seller is going to reject my offer because I just want to make sure I didn't miss something.

Steps to Take When Working Directly with the Seller and It Looks Like a Good Deal

If the seller has some motivation and is looking for significantly less than what I think the after-repair value of the property is, then I call the seller back and confirm or make an appointment to see the property.

Steps to Take When the Property Is Listed by a Real Estate Agent

If I am analyzing a property that is listed by an agent, it is usually only because it is a short sale, a Real Estate Owned (REO), or some sort of distressed property. Thus, I will prepare to go look at the property in person and confirm or make an appointment with the agent to see it.

STEP 7: CLASSIFY YOUR LEADS

Running comparables is the litmus test to figure out if the deal has potential. We then classify and rate the lead: it's either a hot lead, a warm lead, a dead lead, or an agent referral lead.

On *hot leads*, which have plenty of equity, we call back and schedule appointments to see the properties. If the seller is behind on payments and there is no equity, then we know we will have to negotiate a short sale with the bank. A *short sale* is when the mortgage amount is more than the home's market value, and the bank allows the seller to pay less than what is owed to pay off the mortgage. With these types of sellers, we spend about 15 minutes on the phone explaining the short-sale process and all the documents the seller will have to put together for us to be able to negotiate a short sale with the bank. These are hot leads because the bank discounts can be significant, giving us high profits later.

On *warm leads*, we don't make an appointment; instead we call the seller or agent and make a verbal offer. If they don't think our verbal offer is in the zone of possible agreement, then we reclassify the lead as an *agent referral lead* (if the property is not already listed) or a *dead lead* if it is already listed in the MLS.

A lot of deals never make it to Stage 3. When we evaluate 20 properties, we might schedule appointments to look at three or four of them after running comparables. Along the way, we track all this information, saving all the comparables and making notes in our CRM/database.

The CRM (Client Relationship Manager) system is very powerful and allows us to automate our business. Many of our students use our CRM system to grow and scale their businesses. In fact, many have gone from just a few deals annually to multiple deals per month by utilizing our CRM technology.

STEP 8: PREPARE YOUR COMPARABLE PACKAGE

If you have determined the property is worth going to look at in person, then you will want to assemble all your information into a *comparable package*. You will use the comparable package and the information contained within to finish your after-repair-value appraisal at the property and outside the comparables.

Comparable Package

1. *Seller lead sheet:* A copy of the seller lead sheet/script you may have used to gather information from the seller about the property and the seller's situation.
2. *Property card:* A printout of the property card that has details about the property.
3. *MLS listing sheet:* If the property is listed, you want to have the listing sheet printed out with all the property information.

4. *Map of comparable properties:* On most MLSs there should be a map view that plots the comparables you selected and merges that data onto a map that you can print out.

5. *Individual MLS comparable printouts:* You want to print out each individual comparable property you are using to estimate the value of your subject property.

6. *Off-market comparables:* Any additional comparable sales that you found using tax assessor data. You can also use sites like Zillow.com or Trulia to possibly find sold comparables that were not found within the Multiple Listing Service.

7. *Comparable sales adjustment grid:* We use this template Excel spreadsheet to help us determine the after-repair value of the property. This matrix is how we do our property feature comparisons so we can make the proper value adjustments. I discuss this in detail in the next chapter.

8. *Deal analyzer for flips:* I use a template Excel spreadsheet I created to estimate the profit potential of a deal. This helps me formulate an appropriate offer.

9. *Repair estimate sheet:* I use a template Excel spreadsheet to help me estimate the repair cost of a property.

STEP 9: PREPARE YOUR BUYING APPOINTMENT PACKAGE

If you are meeting directly with the seller at the property, then be prepared to put the property under contract during your meeting. Thus, you will want to prepare a *buying appointment package*, which contains all the proper documents and paperwork.

These are important documents you will fill out with the seller if you make a verbal offer that gets accepted. There will be additional paperwork once you go to contract on a property that needs to be filled out before closing; however, it is not necessary the first time you meet with a seller. If the property is a pre-foreclosure, we bring additional disclosures and short-sale-specific documents.

I lost quite a few deals my first couple of years in the business because it took me too long to appraise the property and make my offer. Don't make this mistake; take my advice and be prepared to make an offer on your initial visit to the property.

Buying Appointment Package

1. *Purchase and sale agreement:* This is the contract you will submit to either the listing agent or the seller.

2. *Property disclosures:* These are standard documents you will have the seller fill out that disclose any defects the property may have.

3. *Authorization to release information:* This is a document you will have the seller sign so that you can speak to the seller's bank on the seller's behalf.
4. *Affidavit of purchase and sale agreement:* A document that protects your contractual interest in the property that can be recorded on the land records.
5. *Seller credibility packet:* This is marketing collateral you can give to the seller that contains more information about your company.

CONCLUSION

This second stage of the deal evaluation system gives you the information you'll use to formulate your offer. That's why it's critical that you run your comparables yourself. In my years of experience, investors who make mistakes often make them during this stage of evaluating deals. Track this stage closely.

If a deal still looks viable at the end of the second stage of the deal evaluation system, you're in great shape, and you can move on to the third and final stage of the process: the property visit.

CHAPTER **1 3**

Deal Evaluation System Stage 3

The Property Visit

A dream doesn't become reality through magic, it takes sweat, determination, and hard work.

—COLIN POWELL

I once got a call from a really motivated seller who lived in a good area of town and was only looking for $200,000 for his property. So I ran the deal through the three stages of my deal evaluation system. Stage 1 was smooth sailing. In Stage 2, when I ran the comparables in the area during my desktop evaluation, I found that other properties in the area were all selling for upwards of $350,000.

Obviously, I was pretty excited about this deal. But I never buy a property without first going out to look at it in person. So I got in my car and headed over to the property. When I pulled up to the property, I realized why the seller was only asking for $200,000. His house was literally on the steepest hill I had ever seen and he had no driveway to get up to his front door. I parked on the street and proceeded to climb what felt was like a hundred flights of stairs just to reach the front door. By the time I finally reached the summit, I was literally out of breath.

Needless to say, I didn't put the property under contract that day because the property had a problem I obviously could not fix. However, I did get a good workout.

This story is an example of why it is so important to visit the property you are analyzing before you make an offer. In the third stage of the deal evaluation system, you evaluate the subject property and the comparables in person. If you are dealing with a property that is out of state, you will definitely want someone in the area to follow the exact same steps covered in this chapter.

FILLING OUT THE COMPARABLE SALES ADJUSTMENT GRID

As discussed in the previous chapters, you will be using the sales comparison approach to determine what the after-repair value of the property will be once it is fixed up. Remember, as a wholesaler you earn a profit for finding a good deal and getting the property under contract. You realize your profit by selling the contract or the property itself to another investor who will realize a profit either by rehabilitating the property and reselling it or by keeping it as a rental.

Using the sales comparison approach you will be directly comparing the subject property against three or four recent sales of like-type properties. More specifically, you will be deriving your value by comparing common significant property variables that warrant price adjustments. I created a spreadsheet called the *comparable sales adjustment grid* that has space for the subject property and comparables to be described and compared side by side. This makes it very easy for me to determine the after-repair value of a property and make my adjustments based on the properties' differences. A copy of my comparable sales adjustment grid is given in Figure 13.1. You can also download a copy of the comparable sales adjustment grid by visiting www.TheWholesalingBible.com.

I usually fill out the grid for the subject property and the comparable sales as completely as I can before I head out to look at the properties. A lot of this information can be garnered from the property card or from the listing sheet if the property is listed on the Multiple Listing Service. You will not be able to make all your comparisons and adjustments, though, until you drive by the properties. This is when you will fill out the rest of the information and make your final adjustments.

PERFORMING DRIVE-BY INSPECTIONS OF THE SUBJECT PROPERTY AND COMPARABLES

When I head out to look at the properties I always drive by the subject property first and get a feel for the general neighborhood, the street, and the houses closest to the subject property. I also start filling out any information that is missing on the comparable sales adjustment grid.

I will then drive by the sold comparables before I come back and finish my appraisal on the interior of the subject property. As I visit each comparable I first determine what three or four comparables are the best properties to use as after-repair-value comparables. It is pretty common that I will eliminate from one to four of the comparables at

Comparable Item	Subject Property	Comparable 1 Description	$ + or (-) Adjust	Comparable 2 Description	$ + or (-) Adjust	Comparable 3 Description	$ + or (-) Adjust	Comparable 4 Description	$ + or (-) Adjust
Address									
Sale Price									
Price/Gross Living Area									
Distance to Subject									
Sale Terms									
Sale or Financing Concessions									
Date of Sale/Time									
Location									
Neighborhood									
Street Traffic									
Surrounding Properties									
School District									
Lot									
Lot Size									
Lot Layout & Setbacks									
View									
Exterior									
Exterior Property Condition									
Style of Property & Appeal									
Quality of Construction									
Age of Property									
Landscaping									
Garage/Carport									
Porch/Patio/Deck/Fireplace									
Pool/Fence									
Interior									
Interior Condition									
Square Footage									
Basement & Finished Below Grade									
Functionality of Layout									
Bedrooms									
Baths									
Heating & Cooling									
Energy Efficiency									
Net Adjustment Total		( ) + or ( ) -	$	( ) + or ( ) -	$	( ) + or ( ) -	$	( ) + or ( ) -	$
Adjusted Sales Price of Comparables			$		$		$		$
After Repair Value of Subject Property	$								

FIGURE 13.1   Comparable Sales Adjustment Grid

this point because I realize they aren't the best comparables to use. Remember, you are ultimately trying to determine what the subject property will be worth once it is fixed up. This is very different from trying to appraise the property in its as-is condition. As a wholesaler you have to show a rehabber that he or she can make a profit from the transaction by adding value to the property.

After I have chosen the best comparables I then complete the comparable sales adjustment grid by making adjustments on the grid based on common attribute differences between the properties. The only final adjustments I have to make at this point will be when I return to the subject property to inspect the interior.

EXAMINING COMPARABLES THAT ARE ACTIVE AND ON DEPOSIT

After I have driven by the comparables that have sold I then drive by the comparable properties that are currently on deposit followed by properties that are actively for sale. I occasionally make additional adjustments if I notice something very unusual about these properties.

For example, if a neighborhood has an unusually large number of properties currently for sale, I am definitely going to want to do further research. If this is the case, I go back and look at the neighborhood trends over the last year or two to get a feel for what is common when it comes to the supply. Prices are always affected by the supply and demand of the market, and any time the supply is higher than the demand prices will adjust downward. A balanced real estate market is considered to have six months' worth of supply, so if you are aware of this you can better predict how the supply will affect the after-repair value of the property you are analyzing.

By the time I return to the subject property I have a very good feel for what the after-repair value of the property will be. After you have walked through a lot of houses you will be able to almost predict what the interior of the house will look like based on the condition of the exterior, the style of the property, the square footage, and the number of bedrooms and baths. Of course, if the property is listed, you will probably have already seen interior pictures of it, which makes this step a lot easier.

As you walk through you will generally have a few minor adjustments to make; however, since most of the work was done before you set foot in the property you should feel confident enough to make your offer on the spot if you are meeting with the seller directly. If you are meeting an agent, you will probably call the agent back later that day to make your offer.

MAKING ADJUSTMENTS

Of course, there will always be differences between the subject property you are analyzing and the comparables even in subdivisions built by the same builder. The accuracy of your after-repair-value estimate relies on the categories you selected for the adjustments and the amount of any adjustments you make. It is important to note that the adjustments you make to the value of each property are not simply the cost to construct that feature, but rather what a buyer is willing to pay for the feature. These adjustments for property feature differences should always be based on the demands of the buyers within the market. Ultimately, the adjustment value made will depend on the price points of the properties you are examining, the market you are in, the relative differences between the properties, and so forth.

I believe the categories listed on my comparable sales adjustment grid are the most significant factors to consider when comparing properties. For each comparable you examine you will want to compare the following components of the property listed. These components are all part of the comparable sales adjustment grid that I use to calculate the after-repair value of the subject property. These are some common things that warrant adjustments when comparing the subject property to the comparables.

Sale Terms

- *Sales or financing concessions:* If one of the comparables that was sold involved non-standard financing terms in the form of the type of loan, down payment, or terms of the loan, then an adjustment should be made. For example, a buyer may have paid more for a property than it was worth because the seller provided the financing to the buyer with a very favorable below-market interest rate. So pay attention for a property where the seller may have helped financed the purchase, assumed an existing loan, or bought the property "subject to" the existing mortgage.

  You also want to pay attention for comparables that sold that would not be considered arm's-length transactions. For example, if the principals to the transaction are related individuals or corporations, you must assume this affected the terms of the sale. In these situations you will want to exclude the comparable from consideration.

- *Date of sale/time:* Adjustments should be made for comparable sales that are older than six months. Whether you adjust up or down depends on what the market looked like when that property sold compared to the current state of the market.

Location

- *Neighborhood:* Generally most of the comparables that you evaluate will be in the same neighborhood since your radius search is generally within a half-mile of the subject property. However, there can be differences within a neighborhood depending on proximity to landmarks, parks, restaurants, and shopping, and the appeal of the street the property is located on. A property that borders on a nice park is obviously very different from a property that is next to the freeway or an industrial area, so an adjustment should be made in these situations. Likewise, if you are forced to compare properties in different subdivisions (which isn't ideal) that are within the same neighborhood, you will have to make an adjustment based on the differences between the subdivisions themselves.
- *Surrounding properties:* You should always evaluate the condition of the surrounding properties on all sides of the subject property. You should also look at the properties directly across the street from the subject property. If any of these properties are a major eyesore, then you will definitely need to make a downward adjustment to the after-repair value of the subject property.
- *Street traffic:* Heavy street traffic can have a profoundly negative impact on a property's value so you should definitely make an adjustment if the subject property or one of the comparable sales is on a busy street. Most buyers prefer residential properties that are not on busy streets, especially if they have young children.
- *School district:* Adjustments should be made if the comparables are in different school districts because as you know there can be major differences in the quality of differing school districts. This may not be something you typically think about if you don't have children; however, buyers with children will pay a premium to live in an area that has a superior school system.

Lot

- *Lot size:* You will want to pay attention to the size of the lot when you are comparing properties. Buyers generally prefer bigger lots when they are looking to purchase a property. Likewise, you should know the zoning in the area. If you can buy a house where you can subdivide the lot, obviously this would warrant an increase in the value of the subject property.
- *Lot layout and setbacks:* Generally you just want to rate the lot layout and setbacks as good, average, fair, or poor. Buyers don't like houses that are built close to the street or odd-shaped lots with a lot of space that can't be utilized. You should also

pay attention to the grading of the lot, the availability of utilities, and the presence of mature trees and bushes.

- *View:* A property with a view will always draw a premium over properties that don't have views. Be aware of whether the comparables have views.

Exterior

- *Overall property condition:* I generally note the overall exterior condition of each property as good, average, fair, or poor. You will have to envision what the subject property exterior will look like once the property is finished when making your comparisons and adjustments.
- *Style of house and appeal:* The style of the house should generally fit in and be compatible with the other types of houses in the neighborhood. In some regions of the country there are certain types of house styles that draw premiums that you will want to know based on where you live.
- *Age of house:* If you are comparing houses within the same subdivision, there generally won't be much of an age difference because most were probably built by the same builder within a relatively short time frame. A difference in age of 10 or fewer years won't be much of a difference, either. Overall, newer homes draw a premium over older homes because a lot of older homes tend to have outdated design features or fixtures. However, what is most important is the general upkeep of the properties that you are comparing if the age of the properties is similar.
- *Landscaping:* I generally note the overall landscaping of each property as good, average, fair, or poor. Once again, you are going to have to envision how the subject property's landscaping would look once the property is renovated.
- *Garage/carport:* Any garage or carport on the subject property should be compared based on the size and type of construction. If the subject property does not have a garage or a carport, you will definitely want to make an adjustment.
- *Porch/patio/deck:* Amenities like a porch, patio, deck, or other luxury features should be noted and always add to a property's value (although it might not add nearly what it cost to construct it).
- *Pool/fence:* You definitely want to make a note if the property has a pool and a fence. Adjustments for these features will depend on the local market expectations of buyers. In some areas, pools are expected and a definite value-add. In other, colder areas, they are less valuable and some buyers in those areas actually prefer not to have them.

Interior

- *Overall condition:* I generally note the overall interior condition of each property as recently remodeled, good, average, fair, or poor. Once again, you are going to have to envision what the interior condition of the subject property will look like once it is remodeled when you are making your comparisons and adjustments.
- *Square footage:* I usually run comparables within 20 percent of the square footage of the subject property. I will sometime make small adjustments based on the extra square footage between the subject property and the comparables. If you have to go outside this range to find enough comparables, you are definitely going to want to make a bigger adjustment.

  There are sometimes differences in what the property field card says about the properties' square footage and what the Realtor or seller says the square footage is. If there is a difference, you definitely want to investigate the discrepancy. Remember, it is typical to only count above-grade square footage here. However, in a few states you should find out what is considered typical when it comes to counting square footage. For example, in California, where I live, it is typical for homes that are on hills to count below-grade square footage where one of the levels is at least partially below grade. In other areas, this is definitely not the standard.
- *Basement and finished below grade:* If there are below-grade improvements, like having a finished basement, these should definitely be noted and adjusted for.
- *Functionality of layout:* You should know what is currently desirable in the area and whether the subject property has a good flow from one room to another, nice design features, and room sizes that are similar to the comparables. On the properties my company rehabs we always look to improve upon the floor plan if we can. For example, in a lot of older homes builders typically closed off the kitchen. Yet, buyers in today's market like kitchens that are made for entertaining and flow into the living room or dining room. Thus, we are always adapting the layout to the desires of buyers in today's market.
- *Bedrooms:* Ideally, all your comparables have the same number of bedrooms. If they don't, you need to know there is a sliding scale for each additional bedroom a property has. The more bedrooms a property has, the more it is worth; however, each subsequent bedroom is worth less. You would make a bigger adjustment comparing a two-bedroom to a three-bedroom because there is a big difference in price between the two. Obviously, a three-bedroom is much more desirable than a two-bedroom property and you would make a major adjustment in favor of the three-bedroom. However, if you compare a five-bedroom to a six-bedroom property, the value adjustment you make will be less.

- *Baths:* Ideally, all your comparables have the same number of bathrooms. If they don't, you will want to make an adjustment. The size of the adjustment will depend on the comparables you are evaluating. Likewise, each subsequent bathroom value adjustment jump is slightly less as the number of bathrooms increases.
- *Heating/cooling:* You will want to compare the types of heating and air conditioning systems. There are definitely adjustments you will want to make based on the climate of the area and what type of system was installed within the property.
- *Energy efficiency:* Green homes, solar-heating panels, high R-factor insulation, or any other energy-efficient features should be noted and adjusted for.

CALCULATING ADJUSTMENTS

The accuracy of your after-repair-value appraisal will depend on your use of reliable adjustment values. The most important thing to remember is to make your adjustments based on what buyers are actually willing to pay for feature differences and not what the feature differences actually cost to construct.

For example, a roof deck with a built-in outdoor fireplace might be a really nice feature that costs someone $15,000 to construct. However, when that individual goes to sell her property she may only get $3,000 to $5,000 in additional value for having that feature. Your adjustment values are going to be based on market-driven data and what buyers are actually willing to pay. Unfortunately, the value of the same feature will vary based on property types and the overall value of properties in the neighborhoods you are analyzing. This is why it is always a good idea to keep the data from your comparable sales adjustment grids handy on properties you evaluate. This data can help you make intelligent adjustments when you are analyzing future properties.

CONCLUSION

As a wholesaler, you will spend the majority of your time executing marketing campaigns and appraising properties. You could easily be making 15 to 20 offers to get one property under contract, so it's always in your best interest to use a defined process like the deal evaluation system every time you evaluate a deal.

Finding the right deal is a great start, but it's far from the end of the line. In the next chapter, I'll show you how to estimate the repair cost on a property that needs work.

CHAPTER 14

Estimating Repairs on Properties

I'll need my whole lifetime to polish my craft.

—Eva Green

A lot of investors like the idea of wholesaling because they don't have construction experience. They don't want to bother with managing contractors or the construction process. They believe that all they have to become proficient at is finding deals and buyers for those deals.

They are wrong. As a wholesaler you still have to have some knowledge of how to accurately estimate repairs. When you go to sell that property, you will get a lot of construction-related questions and objections from buyers who are looking at your deal—and you will have to be able to answer them.

One of the reasons my partners and I have sold so many wholesale deals over the years is because our buyers trust the repair estimates that we make. They know that we have a lot of experience rehabbing properties, and they're confident that we're estimating the repair costs accurately. Not only do we point out what repairs are needed, but we also take the time to show other investors simple things they can do to greatly enhance the property's resale value. When you can show an investor-buyer the vision of how the property will look when it's finished, you make a lot more deals in the long run. Where others see "trash," you will hopefully see "cash."

Estimating repairs is not about being a perfectionist. Ideally, you should spend 30 minutes or less making your repair estimates on properties that need minimal work, and no longer than two hours on large residential construction projects.

You may not have any construction experience, and that's okay. Follow the process I outline for you in this chapter and you will gain a basic understanding of what you need to look for when you are estimating repairs. It should also be said that when you fix up properties no set rules apply. Features that are popular in one area of the country may not be popular in another. Today's fads may become tomorrow's paisley wallpaper.

This is why it is so important to have a system, but also perform market research on properties that are selling quickly in your area that have been rehabbed.

REPAIR COST IS A CRITICAL NUMBER YOU NEED TO MAKE THE RIGHT OFFER

In order to make a good offer there are a few critical numbers you need to know. First, you need to know what the after-repair value of the property is. Then, you will deduct the holding and transaction costs for the investor buying the property from you. Then you will deduct the repair cost and your profit. This will leave your *maximum allowable* offer, which is the absolute most you can pay for the property when you are making an offer.

Let's say you are looking at a property that you believe will sell for $200,000 once it is fixed up and the repair cost on the property is $15,000.

After-Repair Value	$200,000
Transaction and Holding Costs (20%)	−$40,000
Repair Cost	−$15,000
Profit	−$10,000
Your Maximum Allowable Offer	$135,000

Remember, your maximum allowable offer is the most you can offer for the property and still make a profit. This should not be your opening offer because you should always leave room to negotiate upwards just a bit. In this example I would most likely open with an offer from $120,000 to $125,000, depending on the situation and the unique variables of the deal.

OUR SYSTEM TO ESTIMATE REPAIRS

To streamline the process of estimating repairs we use what we call a *repair estimate sheet*. This document helps you estimate repairs quickly and accurately and it doesn't take you a long time to complete. To download a copy you can use go to www .TheWholesalingBible.com.

It should be noted that a repair estimate is only a high-level overview of what needs to be fixed on a property. On the properties we choose to rehab instead of wholesale we fill out a much more detailed *scope of work* that outlines everything that will be done to the property that we give to our contractors. This detailed scope of work includes all the materials we want installed in the property and takes us from two to four hours to complete.

EXTERIOR REPAIRS

When I begin the process of estimating repairs I prefer to start analyzing the exterior of the property first.

Roof

This is one of those major areas of the house that you must inspect for damage. If the roof leaks, the buyer you are going to sell the deal to will have to fix it, so make a note of it. Here is what you should look for when you are examining whether the roof needs to be repaired, replaced, or left alone:

- *Replace* the roof when it has more than two layers of shingles on it. In many building codes across the country they do not allow more than two layers of shingles due to weight.
- *Replace* the roof when the shingles are cupping or curling. If, when you stand back from the house to view the roof, you see shingles that are not lying flat, that is a tell-tale sign that the roof is nearing the end of its useful life.
- *Replace* the roof when it looks so bad from the exterior that anyone buying would absolutely determine that they couldn't live with the current roof.

What to Look For

- Look under the eaves for rotten starter board. This tells you the roof is leaking or has leaked in the past.
- Look for shingles that are a different color. This tells you the roof has been repaired in the past.
- Look for leaks in the interior ceilings of the house.
- Roofers estimate a roofing job by how many squares the roof needs. A *square* for roofs is a 10×10 area or $100\ \text{ft}^2$ so make sure you know the lingo.

Gutters

Gutters can have a huge long-term impact on the longevity of a property. Most people don't realize that houses with bad foundations, damp basements, and water issues typically start from bad water management. Gutters help catch and push water away from the house. Buyers looking at your deal will ask you why the basement is damp or taking in water, or why the foundation is settling. You, being a very smart wholesaler, can answer and say that the previous owner did not apply proper water management. Adding gutters and redirecting water away from the house will solve the issue.

There are many different types of gutter materials, including aluminum, plastic, copper, cast iron, and wood. There are also different-shaped gutters, including half-round, box, square-line, and K-style gutters.

What to Look For

- Are there gutters on the property and are they seamless?
- Does the entire house have gutters, or are they just where people enter and exit the house?
- Are the gutters damaged or rusted?
- Do they divert water 24 inches away from the house?

Siding/Stucco

When you have to replace siding or stucco, it is a great opportunity to really change the appearance of the house. You can replace, repair, or just paint the existing material depending on what type of siding or stucco the property has.

House-siding materials have varied over the years and include wood, asbestos, aluminum, vinyl, hardboard composite, Fiberglas, and cement fiber siding.

What to Look For

- The appearance, condition, and type of siding material on the house.
- Stucco that comes in contact with the ground (dirt) will bubble and flake away over time.

Windows

This is an area that you will definitely want to inspect and whether you budget for replacement windows will really depend on the price point of the neighborhood you are in. At a minimum you will want to budget for replacing any broken panes, torn screens, broken pulleys, and damaged frames or sills. The easiest way to look for these is to walk the house and see if the windows lift up and down easily. On most of the houses we wholesale we will budget to replace older windows with dual-pane windows. New dual-pane insulated windows can be considered a selling feature to a new buyer as they reduce heating and cooling bills while keeping out the elements.

Note that landlord buyers cannot get subsidized or Section 8 rentals approved unless they have fully functional and operable windows that are not peeling or cracking.

What to Look For

- What types of windows do the neighbors have? If most neighbors have newer dual-pane windows, then you should replace the windows.
- Open and close a few windows to see how they operate.
- Make sure all windows and sliding glass doors have screens.

Paint

Paint can certainly improve the look of practically any property on the exterior and interior. Almost every home you wholesale will require painting of some sort.

What to Look For

- Any time there are really odd colors used in a home you will want to budget in a cost to repaint. Neutral colors are the safest colors to use when rehabbing a property.

Garage Repair

Repairing a garage is typically a job that you don't want to overestimate. You are generally best served to just factor in a repair cost that would cover cleaning the garage out, some simple repairs to the door or the opener, and new paint. The only time I would suggest otherwise would be if you are estimating repairs on a high-end property or if the garage is a very large focal point from the front of the property.

If the property has a detached garage that is practically falling over, you might consider demolishing the garage. You will definitely want to look at the value of having a detached garage before you rebuild it. In many areas of the country it may not make sense to rebuild a detached garage if the house is in a lower-end area. This will depend on what you see when you pull your comparable sales of like-type after-repair-value properties.

What to Look For

- Does the house have a swing-up garage door or a roll-up garage door?
- Does the door have an opener and does it actually work?

- Is the garage door dented beyond repair and does it need to be replaced?
- Is there any electrical work that needs to be done to the garage?
- Is there any termite damage in the garage?

Landscaping

Almost every property you estimate repairs on will need something factored in for land-scaping. New landscaping has a dramatic effect on how many showings a house will get and ultimately how quickly it sells. It's amazing what simple things like mulch, new bushes, and laying some new grass or sod can do to the appearance of the front of a house.

The best thing about landscaping is it can be very affordable and only takes a few days to complete on most median-price-point homes with smaller lots.

What to Look For

- Keep it clean and green.
- Simple basic landscaping is fine.
- Suggest to a buyer installing planter boxes around the perimeter of the house. It is always important to keep vegetation away from the house.
- Bark planters and mulch around trees gives them a really nice look.

Pools

I have repaired pools, filled in pools, and, of course, cannonballed into pools. The value of having a pool will vary greatly depending on what area of the country you live in. In most areas of the country they are a nice amenity and increase the value of the prop-erty. However, in colder-weather climates some buyers consider pools to be a hassle because they are costly to maintain.

Pools can also be costly to repair if they are not working properly so always test the pool to make sure everything is working properly. If the pool isn't working properly, call a pool repair company to come and give you a more detailed estimate.

What to Look For

- Look closely at a pool that is filled with water. Look for patches of plaster missing.
- Turn the pump on to make sure it is working correctly.
- If the pool is empty, walk in it and look for cracking in the plaster. (If the plaster is cracking, the pool structure is cracked, needing major repair.)
- An empty pool may need to be re-plastered.

Fences

Whether you budget for the fence will depend on the condition of the existing fence and whether the surrounding properties have nice fences. In low-end areas there are times where I do not budget for this item because everyone has an ugly fence. However, in most areas having an attractive fence is a must and it can be repaired, replaced, or installed very inexpensively.

What to Look For

- Look for the easiest fix. Just because the fence is leaning or falling over doesn't mean it needs to be completely replaced. A few new posts and paint can make an old fence look brand-new.

Decks

Decks can be a great addition to any house. On homes that don't have a deck you might consider factoring in the cost to add one. On existing decks see if you can just refinish the deck without having to replace it.

What to Look For

- The height of a deck can add significant costs.
- A good deck will extend the interior living space to the exterior.
- Unless the house is very high-end, use paint-grade wood. Paint the deck surface two shades lighter than the body color of the house and paint the railing the same color as the trim color of the house.

INTERIOR REPAIRS

Once I have completed my estimate on the exterior of the property I then move inside the house to continue my analysis.

Kitchen

The kitchen is the most important area in the interior of the house to most buyers. Buyers who walk into a house and love the kitchen almost immediately envision themselves living in the house. When you can get buyers to this point you are one giant step closer to procuring an offer from them.

However, some rehabbers don't know how to improve the kitchen without breaking the bank so it is your job as a wholesaler to point them in the right direction. In order to do this you should first identify whether the existing kitchen has the proper layout. Then look at the condition of the kitchen and decide what you are actually going to replace.

Layout

The first thing you should always look to do in older homes is see if you can open up the kitchen so it flows into any connecting rooms. Most buyers prefer the kitchen to be open and airy and removing walls is one of the easiest ways to make the home seem bigger without adding any additional square footage to the property. A lot of older homes and mass-produced properties in older subdivisions were built with a separate kitchen, a separate dining room, and a separate living room or living space. These old layouts often feel like a mouse maze, seem claustrophobic, and tend to make the house feel smaller. In these homes one of the easiest and most inexpensive ways to improve the flow of the property is to open up walls and create a "great room" by combining the kitchen with the living room, dining room, or both.

Today's buyers enjoy having the kitchen feel a part of common living spaces so they can entertain and socialize with their guests while still being in the kitchen. It is generally very easy and inexpensive to remove a wall and it can totally change the appeal of the entire interior. Obviously, you will want to know if the wall is load-bearing and, if it is, you will want to budget for an additional support beam.

If the kitchen needs to be completely gutted, then you may have another opportunity to maximize space by changing the layout of the cabinets and appliances. You can easily measure the kitchen, map out the current layout on graph paper, take some pictures, and make a trip to Lowes or Home Depot and have one of their kitchen designers create a new layout for you. This new layout is something you can show to potential buyers who are thinking about making an offer on the property you are wholesaling. Remember, it is your job as a wholesaler to recognize and point out to your buyers things they can do to enhance the value of the property.

Condition

What you do to a kitchen depends on the price point of the property and what the kitchens look like in the other sold and active comparables. It is very easy to spend too much when you are remodeling a kitchen, so make sure you point out what you would do to the kitchen to any buyers you are marketing the property to.

Always look to save things where you can, especially on lower-end properties. Maybe you can just get new matching doors and hardware for the cabinets without having to replace all of the cabinets. Maybe you can reuse some of the appliances. If this is the case, you should point out these money-saving ideas to your buyers.

However, in most properties, reusing materials probably isn't an option if you want your property to stand out so you will have to factor this into your repair estimate. Here are some tips when deciding what to keep, what to repair, and what to replace:

1. Check the sold comparables you are using and make a list of the materials, conditions, and amenities in the other properties' kitchens that you will be competing against.
2. Once you have the list from the comps, check your subject property and determine what it needs to make it competitive at your suggested sales price.
3. Only reuse and keep cabinets, appliances, and countertops if they can compete with the condition and quality of the current houses for sale. When done incorrectly, painting old cabinets just looks like old, painted cabinets. The proper preparations and improvements in the kitchen are vital to anything you decide to keep to rework and reuse.

What to Look For

- Can you keep the cabinets? (Look under the sink; if this cabinet has the most wear and tear and this cabinet still looks good, the rest should be fine.)
- Painting the cabinets or adding new doors and new hardware can make old cabinets look new.
- When changing the layout of the kitchen remember to keep the stove, refrigerator, and sink in a triangle.
- Don't over-think it. If the kitchen is ugly, you will probably have to replace everything.

Kitchen Appliances

Whether you budget for new appliances will depend on the property you are looking at. If you're examining a property and the kitchen needs to be totally redone, then chances are you're going to want to budget for new appliances as well. Finishing a new kitchen or house and leaving old or used appliances is not the smartest thing to do nor should you advise a buyer of yours to do that. The quality of kitchen appliances will also depend on the after-repair value of the home and what other like-type homes have for appliances.

What to Look For

- New appliances go a long way.
- Be careful not to install too-nice appliances in the house.
- Stainless-steel appliances are usually preferred by most buyers.

Bathrooms

In rehabbing, the kitchen and the bathrooms are the two areas of the house that either attract buyers or turn them off. When you are making your repair estimate on a property make sure you spend extra time in these two areas.

The first thing you should look for is whether the house has the appropriate number of bathrooms in comparison to other homes that have recently sold. If you can show a buyer how to add a bathroom on a property that only has one or two bathrooms, it can enhance the value of the property.

Whether the bathrooms need to be completely redone will depend on the property you're looking at. Bathrooms are somewhat easy to replace because most of the time you will just be factoring the cost to replace fixtures.

The master bath is what you should focus on first when you're estimating repairs on a property. If the master bath is small, look for ways to add space or maximize the existing space. Also, look for features that will distinguish the bathroom from other homes. You might consider pointing out to a buyer any of the following:

What to Look For

- Adding a rain-showerhead and/or body-sprays adds a really nice touch to a simple bathroom.
- If the tub needs to be replaced, suggest using a Jacuzzi tub. Buyers fall in love with the bathroom for this reason alone.
- If you're redoing the tile or tub surround, add an accent tile.
- Consider installing a glass shower door as opposed to just putting up a new curtain.
- If there is room to have a double sink, suggest that to your buyer and factor it into your repair estimate.

Flooring

Flooring can definitely make a house stand out and there are plenty of options you can choose from. We have found the best flooring combination that buyers like is hardwood in the living areas, tile in the bathrooms and kitchen, and carpet in the bedrooms. However, if the house is very small, breaking up the flooring like this can make the house appear smaller.

We rehabbed a house recently where the kitchen area was extremely small so we decided not to use tile in the kitchen because it would have been a very small tile floor. Instead, we installed the same hardwood we had used in the living room because the living room connected to the kitchen. This was a smart choice, because when the house was finished it didn't appear as small as it was. We got a full-price offer on the house and the buyers even remarked on how they loved the flooring and how we used hardwood in the kitchen.

What to Look For

- What can you keep? In most houses built prior to 1960, you can sand and refinish the existing hardwood floors.
- Determine a flooring plan that you can show to your buyers. This plan should tell potential buyers what type of flooring you would put in each room.

Sheetrock/Drywall

If the property needs work done on the electrical, plumbing, or heating, then chances are you will also have to replace a lot of the sheetrock. Look at the existing mechanicals before you estimate a repair cost for any sheetrock/drywall. If the property doesn't need mechanical work, then you should walk around all the rooms inside the property and look for sheetrock that is damaged and needs to be patched.

What to Look For

- Pay special attention if the property has a finished basement and is damp. We have bought a lot of homes where we had to completely replace all the sheetrock in the basement because there was mold on or behind the sheetrock in homes that had water problems.
- Look for bad taping jobs that might have to be refinished where you can literally see the seams between pieces of sheetrock. We have seen this a lot on homes where the homeowners tried to redo the sheetrock themselves.
- Look for water damage on the ceilings underneath bathrooms on two- and three-story houses. This is especially common on rental properties with tenants who don't always report water damage to the landlord.

- If the house is made of brick, look for areas you could suggest to a buyer to remove the sheetrock and show the exposed brick. This is a really nice feature a lot of buyers like if the brick is in good shape.

MECHANICALS

As you analyze the interior you also will want to analyze all the major mechanical systems of the property.

Plumbing

As you inspect a property you should always ask the seller and/or agent what type of plumbing they have and if there are any plumbing problems. Also, ask them if there have been any plumbing leaks in any areas of the house. In some properties this will be obvious because you will see watermarks on the ceiling and/or on the flooring. Always pay attention to the first-floor ceilings underneath bathrooms on the second floor. Also, pay attention to the flooring around the kitchen and in bathrooms. However, a lot of plumbing problems will not be so obvious when you are inspecting the property so make sure you always ask questions and test the plumbing.

Discretionary plumbing problems can be fixed by improving the drain lines in the kitchen from 2 inches to 3 inches for better long-term drainage and usage.

What to Look For

- You will always spend money on plumbing. You will be changing out wax rings on toilets, angle stops, supply lines, and ABS drain lines. These are the easy things to see.
- When you are inspecting vacant houses in cold-weather states, *always* test the plumbing because frozen pipes can be very costly to replace.
- You should always look for plumbing that may have been stolen on homes that are vacant. I have walked through a lot of homes where someone stole all the copper plumbing.

Electrical

Lighting can change the entire look and feel of a home when it is done properly. Adding the proper lighting in the kitchen and around the house can really make the house much more appealing.

What to Look For

- On single-family houses always look at the main service panel. If the main panel disconnect is less than 100 amps, you should budget to do a service panel upgrade to 200 amps.
- When you are making your repair estimate, count on having some electrical work that needs to be done. At a minimum you should budget to change all the outlets, switches, faceplates, and many of the lighting fixtures.
- Just because the house is not grounded doesn't mean you need to rewire it.
- On some homes you might suggest to your buyer to add under-cabinet lighting. This really makes the kitchen "pop" when a retail buyer walks through the property.
- Recessed lighting throughout is a nice selling feature and an upgrade you might consider suggesting to a potential buyer.
- Low-voltage lighting with dimmers is also a great touch to help show and sell houses.

HVAC

With heating, ventilation, and air conditioning it is important to always have a clean or up-to-date system in the property you are looking at. If you don't have this, then you may need to consider budgeting for these items.

What to Look For

- There are many different types of heating systems so you have to know what type of heating system is in the house you are looking at. These include forced air, radiant heat, hydronic (hot-water baseboard), steam radiant, and geothermal.
- If the heating system, AC condenser, or water heater is not working properly, then you will need to replace it. These items are not very expensive to replace but can scare away a lot of neophyte investors who might be looking at your deal.

OTHER

Finally, there are a few other ancillary items you will definitely want to take into account when you are estimating repairs.

Permits

A lot of new buyers will ask you whether they should pull permits for work that needs to be done to the house. It is important that you educate buyers on the importance of pulling permits and why they should never cut corners even on small renovation jobs. Anybody who doesn't pull permits will eventually get caught. Once you're flagged by the building department as someone who cuts corners it makes all your future renovation projects more difficult. This is *never* a good thing because a solid relationship with your local building department and building inspectors is something all investors should work hard to foster.

As for costs on permits, this varies across municipalities and will depend on what area of the country you live in. So get familiar and understand the process and costs for pulling permits so you have an answer the next time a potential buyer asks you a question on this topic.

Dumpsters

When you are estimating the cost to repair a property you will always have trash that needs to be removed. This will require that you factor in the cost for getting a dumpster or multiple dumpsters, depending on the size of the project. Removing overgrown landscaping is also one of the easiest ways to enhance the look of a property and increase the value.

Properties that have overwhelming amounts of trash you might even consider pre-habbing. *Pre-habbing* is when you actually close on the property and clean it out before you remarket and sell the property to another investor. It is a cross between a wholesale deal and a rehab.

We discovered this strategy accidentally, nine years ago, when we bought a two-unit fire-damaged property that was literally filled with trash. If you have ever seen the show *Hoarders*, envision that coupled with a fire on the second floor.

We initially tried to wholesale the property; however, we only got one offer for it. We decided not to take the offer because we felt the property had more potential, so we closed on the property and began the rehab process ourselves. Over the course of a few days we filled three 30-yard dumpsters as we cleaned the place out.

When the property was opened up and free of trash it looked a hundred times better and you could begin to see its true potential. Just before our carpenters were about to start framing, my business partner, Paul, and I decided we would send out one more e-mail to our buyers' list to see if anyone wanted to make us an offer on the property. That same day, we got an all-cash offer from another investor that was $20,000 higher than the previous offer we got before we cleaned out the property. We were shocked because all we did was spend about $3,000 cleaning the place out. We realized it was hard for people to envision how the property could finish when they were literally walking through a place that looked like it had been hit with a bomb.

Over the past nine years we have pre-habbed and sold multiple properties. It's not something we do very often because most properties don't require it. However, it is something to consider when you run across a property that is a complete disaster.

Miscellaneous

When you are estimating the repairs on a property you should always factor in a miscellaneous cost for repairs you did not expect.

What to Look For

- The older the house, the more unknowns you will have and the larger the miscellaneous cost you should factor in.
- On larger projects you will definitely want to factor in a larger miscellaneous cost.

THINGS THAT CAN GREATLY ENHANCE THE VALUE OF A PROPERTY

Remember, wholesaling is about finding a bargain opportunity that you sell to a bargain hunter. Part of how you earn your profit is by pointing out to buyers things they can do to enhance the value of the property beyond just replacing fixtures within the house.

The following are a few things we have done in the past on properties we have rehabbed that were all value enhancements. These are possible opportunities for you to consider and make a note of when you are walking through a house on which you are making a repair estimate. These are also things you're going to want to point out to other investor-buyers when you remarket the property.

Create a Better Layout

- Look for opportunities to open up the kitchen so it flows into the living room, dining room, or both rooms, ideally.
- If the front entrance isn't impressive, see if you can remove any of the walls to connecting rooms to make it bigger.
- If the master bedroom is very small, you might consider making it bigger by combining it with a connecting small bedroom, hall closet, or hallway. Only eliminate a bedroom on properties that have at least four bedrooms. I would never go from a three-bedroom to a two-bedroom property just to make the master bedroom bigger.
- Carve out unused space for an office. A lot of people work from home and this can be a big selling feature. You can do this in hallways and in larger rooms.

Add Square Footage

- In higher-priced neighborhoods it may make sense to add square footage. We have bought single-story houses and doubled the square footage by adding a second story. We have also built additions in price points where we know the after-repair value of the property justifies the extra cost.

Add Bedrooms

- In some houses you might consider turning an existing room into a bedroom, or taking an office and adding a small closet so it can be considered another bedroom.
- Look at the existing attic space and see if it is possible to add any bedrooms and take advantage of the extra space.
- Add a bedroom to the first floor if there are bedrooms only on the second floor. Older buyers like first-floor bedrooms. On rental properties you should always consider this because you can get higher rents when you have extra bedrooms.

Add Bathrooms

- If there is only one bathroom, definitely consider adding a second bathroom.
- Ideally you want to have bathrooms on all floors.
- Look for rooms where you can bring the plumbing straight down or up to cut down on the expense of adding a bathroom.
- If you are adding a second-floor bathroom and don't have enough ceiling height, you might consider adding a dormer, especially if you have to redo the roof, anyway.

Finish a Basement

- This won't be a good investment in all areas. But if the basement has plenty of ceiling height and is in an area where the after-repair values support it, this can have a very positive effect.
- If the house is on a hill and you have a walkout basement, then finishing it is definitely something to consider.
- Make an area for a man-cave. Every man needs a cave to call his own, complete with raw meat and his own club (and a big-screen television with the NFL network).

Improve the Landscaping

- Always look for ways to improve the landscaping. This is one of the best investments there is when fixing up a property.

- Look to see if you can put in lighting and give the house a really nice look when potential buyers drive by at night. Lighting can go a long way.

Maximize Storage Space

- Can you maximize the storage space of a house by redesigning closets or installing closets where there are none?
- Consider adding built-in shelving to the living room, dining room, or office.
- In larger kitchens consider putting in an island with cabinet space beneath.
- Open up the stairway or create an access panel beneath the stairs to add extra storage space.

Create Views

- Some houses have amazing landscaping, mountain views, ocean views, or canyon views that the current house does not capture based on its window placement. Identifying where you can change, add, or cut out picture windows can greatly enhance the view.
- Consider adding a raised deck or a roof deck to really capture the views from a property.
- If you have peak ocean, lake, canyon, or valley views, you might consider adding a second story to the property to maximize them.

Eliminate Bad Views

- Put up a high fence to block a neighbor's house that might be an eyesore.
- Consider changing the location of a window that has an unusually unpleasant view.
- Frosting a window if it happens to be in the bathroom can help.

Eliminate Noise

- Adding insulation, caulking, trees, shrubs, and dual-pane or even soundproof windows can reduce or eliminate noise in a house.

Bring in More Natural Light

- Natural light puts a smile on everyone's face. Taking advantage of opportunities to add more natural light will only help the value of and the ability to market your house. You can achieve more natural light by adding enlarged windows, changing solid doors to those with glass, and adding skylights where possible.

Make Good Color Choices

- Using a lighter color palette will visually open up spaces and make them feel larger. Painting dark trim or old wood trim white can have a huge visual impact on a room and space that helps show and sell the house.

CONCLUSION

Estimating repair costs is an area of real estate investing that's hard to teach in a book. You won't become completely comfortable estimating repairs on a property overnight. Take the time to learn how to *rehab* houses—even if you don't plan on doing a lot of them yourself. You should also consider getting a more experienced investor-coach who can double-check your repair estimates on the first few deals you make offers on.

I have seen people try to learn it by reading a book they bought on building houses from Home Depot. However, I know from coaching a lot of investors that the absolute best way to learn how to rehab houses is to go to a property with someone who is very knowledgeable about how to estimate repairs and manage construction projects. We do this with our coaching students over the course of four days at our intensive rehabbing boot camp. Our four-day event is a unique learning environment for investors because we break down exactly what we are doing to the property, what materials we are using, and what the cost is for each section of the property rehab. If you want more information about this event and our coaching program, please visit www .FortuneBuildersMastery.com.

At this stage in the process, you have estimated the repair cost and calculated the after-repair value of the property and are ready to make an offer. In the next chapter you will learn the process I use to negotiate and make offers on wholesale deals.

CHAPTER 15

Negotiating and Making Offers to Sellers

All training is negotiation, whether you're training dogs or spouses.

—IAN DUNBAR

To achieve long-term success as a wholesaler, you need to continually hone and refine your negotiation skills. Almost every wholesale deal you get will require you to negotiate the seller down on his or her price. You also need to be prepared to deal with the unexpected.

Years ago, I negotiated a deal with a husband and wife who were in the middle of a difficult divorce. We were sitting at their kitchen table and discussing the closing timeline. I was having a hard time getting them on the same page and in the middle of the discussion the wife grew so enraged with her husband's words that she grabbed the salt shaker off the table and threw it at his head. I, meanwhile, literally went from negotiating a real estate deal to negotiating World War III.

As I drove away from the meeting that day, I realized how important communication is in any relationship and in any business.

Learning how to communicate and negotiate at a high level is something that takes practice. Anyone can improve his or her ability to negotiate by preparing well, asking the right questions, having the right process to follow, and learning how to build trust and rapport. It is definitely a skill set that you can practice and improve upon as well. In fact, through an entire transaction there will be multiple parties you will end up negotiating with. For example, you may find yourself in negotiation with sellers, Realtors, lenders, contractors, and buyers in any given transaction.

Each interaction you have is an opportunity for you to enhance the profitability of your deal. You just need to know how to negotiate.

NEGOTIATE WITH CONFIDENCE

Often, fear inhibits new investors from initiating a negotiation and prevents more experienced investors from achieving their ultimate goals. But the truth is you have been negotiating your entire life. As infants, we cried to get our way; then we used hand signals, and eventually learned to use our words. We became experts in our teenage years, always evaluating our parents and figuring out what leverage we could use and when to use it. Likewise, you probably negotiate every day whether it's with your spouse, children, friends, and/or family. So, although it can be scary, have confidence that you have been doing it for much longer than you think.

In this chapter I focus on teaching you how to negotiate directly with a seller who is looking to sell his or her property. These same general concepts apply when you are negotiating through a real estate agent on a property listed on the market.

STEP 1: UNCOVER THE SELLER'S TRUE NEEDS AND DESIRES

The first step to setting up a successful negotiation is to develop a process to follow to gather the proper information to appraise the property. In earlier chapters we discussed what information you need to gather in order to evaluate and appraise a property.

At the same time you will want to uncover the seller's true needs, wants, and desires outside of money. Sellers generally want more money for their properties than you will be willing to offer, so you have to look for other ways you can benefit the seller. Here are some vital things you need to know about a seller's situation in order to make a more appealing offer:

- What is the seller's reason or motivation for selling at this time?
- How quickly does the seller want to sell?
- Is the seller experiencing any financial problems?
- Is the seller current on the payments?
- Is the seller facing any other difficult issues in life?
- What is the seller going to do with the property if it doesn't sell?
- Does the seller still live in the property?
- Does the seller have the money or desire to fix up the property?
- Are there any title problems?
- Has the seller found another place to live?
- How long has the seller owned the property?

- What are the seller's expectations?
- Who else has looked at the property?

When you know the answer to these questions you will have a better picture of what is going on with the seller's life and how you can help the seller. It will also help you understand and empathize with the seller's situation so you can hopefully solve some of the problems. If you can connect with sellers and help them solve a few of these issues, they will be much more likely to want to do business with you.

Working with motivated sellers really requires a high level of emotional intelligence. Emotional intelligence is the ability to identify, comprehend, use, and control emotions. This not only comprises your own emotions but also those of others, including the motivations and desires of the sellers you are working with. If you take the time to truly understand them, you will have a better opportunity of influencing them in a positive way. Many sellers over the years have made the choice to work with us simply because we took the time to listen to and empathize with their difficult situation.

From your very first conversation with the seller it is imperative to build trust and rapport. People prefer to do business with people they can trust and who they perceive to be like them. If there isn't a genuine connection between you and the seller, it can be quite difficult to have a positive outcome. Knowing what your seller wants and needs, and structuring your offers around those needs, will give you a distinct advantage while negotiating. Understanding and directly addressing any concerns will allow you to be more successful at obtaining what you ultimately want out of the deal.

STEP 2: RESEARCH THE SELLER OR AGENT
YOU'RE NEGOTIATING WITH

Before you meet the seller or agent you're working with in person you should take the time to conduct some research about them. In this day and age, information is at our fingertips. Finding out basic information about sellers can be as simple as entering their names in an online search engine. Getting a feel for what their interests are can assist you in understanding sellers or agents before even meeting them. In your research, try to get a glimpse at what their life looks like so you have a deeper understanding of their situation. Also, try to find a commonality that you can relate to and utilize to build trust and rapport with the seller. If your seller is active on the web, taking a quick look at her social media profiles will also give you an indication as to what she is interested in as well.

STEP 3: KNOW WHAT YOU ARE OFFERING BEFORE MEETING WITH THE SELLER

A large part of setting your negotiation up for success happens during the due-diligence phase as you are researching and appraising the property. I highly recommend that you don't meet with the seller until you have had time to verify any information the seller told you about the property, pulled comparable sales, and driven by the comparable sales to determine the after-repair value of the property.

Once you have done this, you can crunch the numbers and determine your offer. Knowing what you are going to offer allows you to approach the meeting with the seller with that much more confidence. Of course, you may adjust your opening offer slightly up or down depending on the condition of the interior once you walk through the property.

Having the confidence and knowledge of what you are going to offer will make it that much easier to negotiate with the seller because you will know the outcome you are trying to reach.

STEP 4: WALK THROUGH THE PROPERTY

When you arrive at the property it is important to make a good first impression. You want to make the seller feel very comfortable about the meeting and process you have for evaluating properties and making offers. Sellers are judging you as much as you are judging them, so it is important to give the impression that you are a professional.

After the initial introductions ask the seller to take you on a tour of the property so you can get a feel for the overall condition. Let the seller know that you will be making a repair list as you go and that she should feel completely comfortable letting you know about anything that needs to be fixed or replaced. Also, reassure the seller that, as an investor who works on homes for a living, there is nothing that will scare you away from making an offer.

As you walk through the property, point out anything that is noticeably wrong and get answers to any questions you have about the property. Make sure to take notice of structural problems, broken fixtures or finishes, obviously outdated décor, stains, major wear and tear, and anything broken or unusable, just to name a few. Don't be rude when pointing out the flaws, but be certain that the seller knows you're aware of these flaws because it will help you later in your negotiation. Any repairs that the property may need can be used to establish justification for the offer you will make.

The property walkthrough is vital to your negotiations, because it enables you to see what the interior condition of the property is and what repairs are required. This will help you finalize the offer you are going to make.

STEP 5: BUILD RAPPORT AND DIVE DEEPER INTO THE SELLER'S MOTIVATING FACTORS

Once you've finished the property walkthrough its time to sit down with the seller and gather any final information you need to make an intelligent offer. Ideally, by the time you meet with the seller in person you already have an idea of the seller's motivations. However, this is a great time to dive deeper into the seller's situation and true motivations for selling the property. Hopefully, you have established some rapport with the seller because rapport is the foundation of a good negotiation. It's all about building trust, being sincere, and putting the seller at ease. Keep in mind that unless you've done business with the individual in the past, the seller is inviting a complete stranger into her home. If she has had previous bad experiences with agents or other investors, the seller is likely to be distrustful right off the bat. Therefore, it's crucial that you get the seller to open up and trust you.

It is essential that you ask really good, open-ended questions so that you get the seller to open up. You should be listening more than talking. When you talk to the seller, try to maintain a 30/70 dialogue. In other words, make sure that you're talking 30 percent of the time and the seller is talking the other 70 percent. The natural result is that you'll be listening most of the time, and listening is the best way to understand your seller and develop a good relationship with him or her. You must be an active listener and try to understand the seller's deepest motivations in order to discover the person's needs. Too many wholesalers blow a negotiation because they rushed in and tried to reach a conclusion without really understanding the seller's point of view.

Occasionally, sellers may not divulge all information and may have issues that they aren't being exactly honest about. Although a seller can make you aware of one specific problem, you may uncover other skeletons in the closet as you continue on through the process. For example, they may not only be behind on their mortgage payments, but they could also be going through a divorce, have recently gone through bankruptcy, or a variety of other scenarios. The more you listen, the more likely you are to uncover any, and hopefully all, of the seller's real needs and concerns. Remember, you're not just trying to make a good impression; you're paving the way toward making an offer and getting it accepted. Rapport is your first step toward success.

After you've found any surface-level information that you can open up and speak about, try to dig deeper into the person to find out what you have in common. In order to build a strong relationship, most people relate to topics such as family, occupation, or things they are passionate about. Ask questions based on these topics, such as, "What do you do for a living, if you don't mind my asking?" Asking these kinds of questions allows the sellers to open up and talk about themselves. Finding common ground allows the parties to openly communicate as people rather than as adversaries.

When you are establishing rapport, it's important to remember that your words, tone, and body language all play a part. Try to subtly match your personality and body language to that of the seller. If the seller is excited, be excited! If you notice he or she is more passive and soft-spoken, don't be so aggressive that you cause the seller to retreat into a shell; lower your voice and connect with the person a bit differently. But on the other hand, if a seller is outwardly aggressive, don't be too passive or quiet, causing the person to think twice about your ability to follow through on any assertions you make. The key is to make your sellers feel comfortable. You are trying to send an unconscious message that you are a professional they can like, trust, and respect.

If the seller hasn't yet opened up about his true motivations for selling during the rapport-building phase, the main objective is for you to move the seller to do as much talking as possible. Make sure to ask open-ended questions, listen intently, and remember this conversation so you can take notes and quote as needed later. By showing the seller you are listening intently and generally interested in what he has to say, you will develop an instant rapport. During this conversation, listen closely for hints and suggestions of information that can possibly help you later when you are negotiating terms and sale price. For example, you can ask questions like:

- "What brought you to the point of selling this house?"
- "You said that you're three months behind on your mortgage payments. How did you find yourself in this predicament?"
- "How are you feeling about your move?"
- "What are your worries or concerns about this process?"
- "What is your goal from the sale of this house?"

In addition to finding the seller's motivation to sell, you should also find his reasons for choosing to call you versus a Realtor, or trying to sell the house by himself. These details are important because you will repeat many of these things back to the seller to pre-frame your offer. Likewise, the more you know about the seller's situation, the better prepared you are to handle any questions, concerns, or objections the seller has.

STEP 6: EXPLAIN HOW YOU CAN HELP THE SELLER

Once you have a good understanding of the seller's situation and reasons for selling, you should have a good idea of how you can help him. Remember, your purpose is to help him find a solution to his problem. Once you know the problem, try to understand the desired outcome. A way to elicit this outcome is to find out what it is that the seller values. Is it time, or money, or health, or future security? For example, if your seller is going through a divorce, then this person will more than likely want the process to be quick and painless. Once you determine and understand what is important to the seller, it creates value in your negotiation. And creating value is what ultimately gets the seller to want to do business with you.

Although money may be the first thought that comes to mind when thinking about what the seller is looking for, that isn't always the case. Remember, the buyers with the highest offers don't always get their offers accepted. Always look for other ways that you can help the seller that don't require you to raise your offer.

- *Offer cash:* If you have the ability to make an all-cash offer I would highly recommend you do so. Cash is king and is something that you need to let the seller know the benefits of. A lot of buyers who have to get financing end up taking longer to close and sometimes they end up not being able to qualify for financing. Sellers under tight timelines will definitely see the benefit of all-cash offers.
- *Close on the seller's timeline:* A lot of buyers have a specific timeline for moving into a house. As an investor your timeline is much more flexible. You can close relatively quickly if the seller needs to. A lot of motivated sellers are in financially distressed situations and don't want to or can't make extra mortgage payments. A quick close can be very appealing to a seller. Likewise, a lot of sellers need time to relocate. Obviously, you're not moving into the property, so if a longer timeline is desirable for the seller, you will also be able to accommodate him.
- *Offer to help the seller find a good moving company:* Moving can cause major stress to sellers. Offer to help them figure out what to do with existing appliances and help them get set up with a moving company. This can be a big relief to sellers and something that only requires you to make a few phone calls.

- *Offer assistance with relocation:* If a seller is moving outside of the area, she may not have had the time to locate a new place to live. You could very easily make a few phone calls and find a good Realtor who can help her find an apartment or a home to purchase.
- *Offer to help sellers find a good credit repair company:* A lot of sellers who have financial problems have bad credit. Offer to help them find a good credit repair company that could help them start to repair their credit.

These are just a few examples of ways you can contribute that don't cost a large amount of money or time; however, they *can* be of high perceived value to the seller. You should establish with sellers that there are many other ways you can help them down the road and that you always look to create long-term relationships with people with whom you do business. When you go above and beyond, you stand out from the competition even when your offer is slightly lower.

STEP 7: FRAME YOUR OFFER

When you present your offer you always want to frame it in as positive a light as you possibly can. Obviously, many of your offers will be lower than what the seller wants so you have to summarize briefly all the benefits of working with you so the seller realizes that you can offer him more than just money.

If the property needs a considerable amount of work, you have to summarize and remind the seller about the work the property needs. It is also a good idea to plant seeds of doubt about the health of the real estate market if you can. Likewise, you should remind the seller that you are offering him a solution *now* as opposed to holding out and "hoping" he gets a higher price.

After you have framed your offer, it is time to let the seller know what you are willing to pay. Once you let him know your price, let him talk and pay very close attention to his initial reaction.

STEP 8: HANDLE OBJECTIONS EFFECTIVELY

Objections are a natural part of the negotiation process and can occur at any stage of the game. You'll know you've encountered an objection from a seller by a number of different factors. It could be body language, eye contact, or a flat-out interruption while you're speaking. Sometimes, they tend to seem a little confrontational because they usually take place once an offer has been put on the table, which means that your offer may need to be justified. But as long as you maintain the right attitude, there is no reason to be terrified when a seller has concerns. Instead, recognize that an objection means the seller is still interested and is at least considering your offer. Remember that you are the problem solver, so when objections arise, use the opportunity to add value to your position as the experienced investor.

The first step in handling an objection is to understand what it truly is. Is it really an objection, or is it just a question? Most often, if your offer is fair and holds value, the seller's objection likely stems from an overall lack of understanding, which would require your providing additional explanation to put him at ease. To effectively handle a seller's objections, follow these key steps:

1. *Recognize the objection:* Uncover what is going on underneath the objection before confronting the issue. You can do this by repeating the objection back to the seller to make sure you understood it correctly. You also want to make sure you are recognizing the question by following with a statement such as:
   - "I understand your concern."
   - "I am glad you brought that up and appreciate your thought process."
2. *Compliment the validity of the objection:* You can also recognize the objection in a way that validates the concern and also compliments the person:
   - "That's a really good point you bring up. Let's take some time to address that."
   - "That's a very good question you have; in fact, it's the most common question that I receive."
3. *Answer the question contained in the objection:* You then have to answer the question that was outlined. The way you approach this is very important. You want to make sure you are consulting with the seller and not just talking over the seller. Keep your tone of voice positive and don't act as if you've taken it personally. When you are answering the question, make sure not to talk too much; otherwise, you may fall out of rapport.
4. *Support the answer:* When you provide an answer, you may still face some resistance. In order to keep things moving along, make sure you are able to validate and support your answer as well. This should be natural for you since you've already conducted your research beforehand. Try convincing the seller to see things from your perspective. Make sure you are supporting your answer, and not arguing the seller's rebuttal.

Finally, you need to quickly and effortlessly move on with the process. You aren't avoiding the objection, because you've answered it; you're just avoiding dwelling on that objection.

If you receive too many follow-up objections from the seller, it is usually an indication that you aren't dealing with a very motivated person. If a seller is too combative, don't be afraid to just let the deal go.

STEP 9: SIGN THE PURCHASE AND SALE AGREEMENT

You can't be afraid to close the deal with the seller. If you and the seller have come to terms, I highly recommend that you fill out a purchase and sale agreement at the meeting. You have worked very hard to get to this point so be prepared to sign a contract at this point in the deal.

CONCLUSION

Every negotiation is different, and becoming comfortable in your role as a negotiator takes practice. Don't worry if you don't get the hang of it right away. Successful investors aren't born with all the answers. The key is to practice, practice, practice, and then practice some more.

I frequently have become baffled by a question while meeting with a prospective seller. I would then go back and update my script with the new objections I encountered and the best way to respond. Let's face it—it happens to all of us. But just because you may have a small setback in your negotiations, it doesn't have to mean the end of the road for that deal. You can always respond to the seller with the appropriate answer at a later time, while still moving the negotiation along and locking up the deal.

Refer back to this chapter any time you are about to enter into a negotiation with a seller. This process has worked very successfully for myself and many of our real estate coaching students. Over time it will become second nature to you and become a natural part of your real estate investing efforts.

In the next chapter, we will cover the elements of a purchase and sale agreement so you feel confident explaining it to a seller at the end of the negotiation process.

CHAPTER **16**

Understanding Purchase and Sale Agreements

A successful man is one who can lay a firm foundation with the bricks that others have thrown at him.

—DAVID BRINKLEY

Usually, after you negotiate with the sellers and get them to agree to a price you will memorialize the terms you agreed to by filling out a purchase and sale agreement. The *purchase and sale agreement* is what gives you control of the property. If you plan on selling the contract, these terms are also what you will pass on to your wholesale buyer, so it is important for you to understand all parts of the agreement.

However, there is no standard purchase and sale agreement. This is why it is extremely important to use an agreement you're familiar with. If someone else is drawing up the purchase and sale agreement, you have to make sure you read every clause within the agreement to make sure you're comfortable with it. Although there is no such thing as a standard, what you will find is in most areas investors will use the Board of Realtors purchase and sale agreement that agents use. This is the agreement that most local agents, attorneys, lenders, title companies, and escrow agents will be very familiar with, and that makes this agreement the one that you, too, will typically want to use. If someone else draws up the purchase and sale agreement, you'll need to read every clause in it to make sure you're comfortable with what it says before you sign it.

This chapter breaks down the common components you will find in most purchase and sale agreements.

PARTIES INVOLVED

This section indicates the names of all the parties to the agreement and is usually the first section you will fill out in most purchase and sale agreements. More specifically, this identifies the name(s) of the seller(s) and the buyer(s). It's extremely important that you get all the sellers to sign the purchase and sale agreement; otherwise, it is not valid. I made a huge mistake early in my career where I met with a seller and we came to an agreement and filled out a purchase and sale agreement. Unfortunately, I did not know that his wife was also on title, and two days later the wife called me and told me that she refused to sign the contract. I ended up losing a really good deal because I didn't meet with both parties when I originally struck the deal with her husband.

DESCRIPTION OF REAL ESTATE

This section simply describes what real property is being sold and bought. It identifies the subject property by these three items:

1. Street address, city, state, and zip code
2. Legal description
3. Property description (single-family dwelling; two-family residence)

It's very important to make sure you know exactly what you are buying and that the size of the lot matches the survey. Never assume anything and always verify the lot lines and surveyed boundaries. Pay special attention to any encroachments that you may encounter as you walk the property.

We once bought a property and found out after we closed that the driveway was shared with the neighbor next door, who was a complete jerk. It ended up being a nightmare and delaying the second closing over 30 days.

PERSONAL PROPERTY INCLUDED IN THE SALE PRICE

There is always a section that describes what personal property is included with the sale. Generally, personal property is considered anything that is not attached to the building or the land. For example, curtains, refrigerators, and window air conditioners are all considered personal property; if those things are important to you, then you need to list them in this section on the contract. Never assume something will remain with the property; if it is important to you, then you should definitely list it.

I once did a final walkthrough on a property we were buying and found that the seller had literally stripped the property of everything. The chandelier, ceiling fans, mini-blinds, toilets, hanging lights, and all the appliances were removed from the property. The seller had the right to remove some, but not all, of these items. I ended up having to negotiate at the last minute because I was caught off guard by the situation.

PURCHASE PRICE AND FINANCING

This section is obviously very important to both parties. In the agreement you list out the purchase price, deposits, and the terms of financing.

Usually the agreement will have a series of lines that will add up to your total purchase price so that it is very clear to all parties the size of the deposit, what amount is to be financed, and how much will be required at closing.

Remember, the validity of your purchase and sale agreement is not dependent on the amount of your deposit. Your earnest-money deposit is a sign of good faith, demonstrating that you intend to complete the purchase. Obviously, if you want to make your offer stronger, then you will increase the size of your deposit because it is an indication of your seriousness.

WHERE DEPOSITS ARE HELD

There is usually a section that outlines where the deposits are to be held and the rights of the seller and buyer in respect to the deposits. This section tends to be unique to each state, so check with your attorney to make sure it complies with local regulations. Remember, never give the deposit directly to the seller. Make sure it is always held *in escrow*.

FINANCING CONTINGENCY

In this section of the agreement you will outline any financing details. If you plan on getting financing from a lender, this section will need to be completed with maximum terms of financing you are willing to accept. You should clearly state the amount and the terms of the financing you desire.

Generally, as a buyer, I will simply cross this section out or check off the "Other" box and put in "Cash." Once again, this is to make your offer stronger in the eyes of the seller.

CONDITION OF PREMISES

In most agreements it outlines the condition in which you expect the property to be delivered to you.

INSPECTION CONTINGENCIES

You will want to hedge your purchase and sale agreement by writing in a lengthy inspection contingency. This will give you the legal right to back out of the agreement within the time frame if the condition of the property doesn't meet your standards as written into the purchase and sale agreement. This is also something you will want to leverage to get your contractors, engineer, and buyers into the property prior to closing.

Just be aware that if the seller has a real estate agent, the agent will typically want you to have a shorter inspection contingency than you would want. Typically, the agent will want 14 days or less, so just expect that when there is an agent involved in the transaction.

STATEMENT REGARDING LEAD-BASED PAINT

There are in most agreements disclosures related to houses built before 1978 that might have lead-based paint.

OCCUPANCY, POSSESSION, AND CLOSING DATE

This section of the contract determines your deadline agreed upon for the closing date. You always want to give yourself as much time as possible so you have time to wholesale the property. If the deal is a great one, I will be flexible and close sooner if the seller wants to. Of course, if the deal is marginal and I know that I'll have to work hard to get it wholesaled, I will push for a closing at least 30 to 45 days out. With this point, you have to read the seller and see how flexible he or she can be. This section is always dictated by my exit strategy, the quality of the deal, and the seller's situation. As long as you can close within a reasonable time (a couple of days to a week) of this date, you are within the lawful standards of performing on most contracts.

DEED TYPE

In most agreements you will see a section that refers to the type of deed that is to be conveyed. This will depend on the state in which you are doing business and what is considered typical.

MARKETABLE TITLE

This point is included to give you an option to reject the purchase and regain your deposit in the event the seller is unable to pass clear title to you or you are unable to obtain title insurance due to a lien or encumbrance that comes up in a title search.

ADJUSTMENTS

This section covers any adjustments that will be made at the closing. These adjustments will include taxes, water and sewer charges, and other similar adjustments. These may vary in your state, so refer to your local contract to make these adjustments in the verbiage of this contract.

BUYER'S DEFAULT CLAUSE

In most agreements there is a clause that restates the rights to the seller in case of a buyer's default on the terms agreed upon in the contract. It will typically list out the method of resolution, damages, who bears the expense, and specific performance.

SELLER'S DEFAULT CLAUSE

In most agreements there is a clause that restates the rights to the buyer in case a seller defaults on the terms agreed upon in the contract. It will typically list out the method of resolution, damages, who bears the expense, and specific performance.

RISK OF LOSS AND DAMAGE

There will usually be some sort of clause that protects your interest in the event of damage to the property while you have it under contract. It also grants you an option of exercising your right to purchase the property in the event of a fire or other significant damage and receive insurance proceeds for such damage.

ADDENDUMS

There is usually a section that covers any addendums and common disclosures included with the contract.

BROKER/AGENT FEES

There is usually a paragraph in most contracts where you can disclose both the agency relationship with the selling broker and the amount of commission he or she will receive. There will also be a section for the buyer's agent and the amount of commission he or she is to receive.

TIME TO ACCEPT

There is usually a clause that simply states how long the offer is valid for the seller to accept it.

CONCLUSION

When you know what's in your purchase and sale agreement, you put yourself in a position of confidence and trust. You are fully aware of your rights. You are able to explain the different clauses within the contract, and you have the knowledge to ease the minds of nervous sellers. You are equipped to handle this stage of wholesaling smoothly. The only way to do this effectively, though, is to know what each section of the contract means and what objections or concerns the seller may have about each part of the agreement.

With the purchase and sale agreement signed, the property is in your control for the first time. Now you can start the process of turning it into profit for your business. In the next chapter, I'll show you how to get the money to fund your wholesale deals.

CHAPTER 17

How to Get the Money for Your Wholesale Deals

Whether you're brand-new to wholesaling or a seasoned professional, there is one thing every deal needs: *money*. You need money to grow your real estate business— that's a given. What not everyone realizes, however, is that it doesn't always have to be *your* money.

There are two common ways to earn a profit when you are wholesaling. You can either sell the contract, often referred to as *assigning the contract*, or you can *double close*, often referred to as a *back-to-back closing* or a *double escrow*.

Obviously, if you plan on selling the contract, you won't be selling the property; so you won't need funding to purchase the property. This is an ideal way to get started wholesaling properties if you don't have a lot of capital or access to other sources of funding. In this scenario, the buyer you sell the contract to will be the one who actually closes on the property.

However, there are many scenarios where you will be better off double closing, or will have to double close. I discuss these scenarios in detail in later chapters in this book. What's important to know is that as a wholesaler you can't always count on being able to sell the contract on every deal. Thus, it is important to secure funding for your deals before you start making offers. I do not advise you to start wholesaling without having at least one source of funding lined up in case you have to double close on the property. Therefore, you need to be aware of the different funding sources available to you.

You will want to build relationships with specialty/niche lenders who understand wholesaling and can provide short-term funding for properties you will close on and resell. The best three sources for short-term funding will be private-money lenders, transactional lenders, and hard-money lenders. There are, of course, other sources of funding beyond these three; however, these are the sources that are most readily available for individual investors who are wholesaling regularly. Over the years these have been the three sources of financing I have used most often to fund wholesale transactions.

Likewise, you will want to refer your end-buyers to your financing sources so they can purchase wholesale properties from you on a continuous basis. As you know, conventional mortgage lending guidelines are stricter these days, making it more difficult for investors to obtain traditional financing—often, even with large down payments.

CONCLUSION

Every transaction will be different. That's why you need to understand the pros and cons of the many funding options available to you. Line up at least one of these funding sources before you start making offers on properties. You can even decide to line up multiple sources from day one, which gives you more options and deeper pockets.

Finally, the cost of the money isn't what counts the most—it's the *availability* of it. In the end, the lender has to earn a profit, as well. In the next few chapters, I will take you through the three most common sources of funding for your back-to-back wholesale deals, starting with negotiating with and making offers to sellers.

CHAPTER 18

Working with Private Lenders

*A bank is a place that will lend you money if you can prove that you don't
need it.*

—Bob Hope

When my partners and I started our real estate business over a decade ago, we had
to learn how things worked from the ground up. But there was one thing we caught
onto pretty quickly: the power of leveraging private money.

By the end of our first year in business, we had lined up close to $2 million in com-
mitments from a handful of private lenders. The effect was staggering. The number of
offers we made on a weekly basis tripled, and our growth as a business shot through
the roof.

If your wholesale transaction requires funding, private money is the single best
source of it. It's also the best source of funding for properties that you decide to rehab.
About 70 percent of all of our real estate transactions have been financed using at least
some private money over the years.

Private lenders allow you to borrow what you need at lower interest rates with
flexible terms. You don't have to spend a lot of time jumping through hoops trying
to qualify for loans with banks or other lenders—and risk losing deals in the process. Lining up private money lenders gives you the confidence you need to make
a greater number of offers, as well as flexibility in the exit strategies you choose
to utilize.

Over the years, my business partners and I have made millions flipping properties and we have found private lending to be a great way to keep earning high rates of
return on our money. Instead of letting our money sit in the bank at dismal interest
rates, we've learned how to lend our money for much higher rates of return to other
investors.

WHAT EXACTLY IS "PRIVATE MONEY"?

A *private money loan* is similar to a bank mortgage, except that an individual rather than a financial institution or a government-backed agency, such as Fannie Mae or Freddie Mac, provides the money for the loan. The property itself is used as collateral for the loan, just like a bank, except private money lenders don't usually report to the credit agencies.

Private money loans are typically short-term loans ranging from one day to a couple of years, depending on the type of real estate transaction. As a wholesaler you will usually be borrowing private money for 1 day to up to 120 days, depending on the length of time you hold the property.

Private money interest rates and points are completely negotiable and determined by what you and the lender agree upon. Typically, private money lenders charge anywhere between 6 and 15 percent annual interest. Some private money lenders charge points and some don't. A point is 1 percent of the loan amount that is paid upfront or in arrears.

If you plan on using private money lenders to fund short-term wholesale transactions, you will definitely want to offer them points. I believe 1 to 3 points is fair, depending on the length of time you hold the property. The reason you will offer a private lender points on a wholesale deal is because you are utilizing their money for only a very short period of time. Since the interest is prorated to the day, a private money lender won't earn enough money if he gets his money back within a few days. That is why you will offer the lender points so that it is worth his time to investigate the deal and lend you the money.

HOW IS THE LENDER PROTECTED?

The private money lender will want you to sign a promissory note agreeing to the terms that you and the lender agreed to. This note can be a mortgage or a deed of trust, depending on the laws of the state you are buying the property in.

In *title-theory* states, a mortgage is used. This means the lender holds the title, a legal document establishing ownership of the property, and it transfers to the borrower when the loan is paid in full.

In *lien-theory* states, a mortgage is also used, but the borrower holds the title. In these states a lien is recorded against the property. The lien is removed when the borrower pays the lender off in full.

Finally, some states are *deed-of-trust states*. A deed of trust is very similar to a mortgage, but the title is held by a third-party trustee and given to the borrower when the loan is paid in full.

In all cases the lender is protected because he has a loan that is secured by the property itself. If the borrower defaults, the lender could foreclose on the property just like a bank.

Private money lenders will also want you to get title insurance even though you may only own the property for a few days. Likewise, private money lenders will want you to get property insurance and they will want to be named as a *loss payee* in case something bad happens to the property.

Finally, some private lenders will want you to personally guarantee the loan, which means they could lay claim to your assets in case you default on the loan. This, of course, is completely negotiable depending on the private money lender you are working with.

TURNING PEOPLE INTO PRIVATE MONEY LENDERS

Finding private money is not nearly as difficult as people think. In fact, anyone with money can be a prospect. In many cases, private money lenders may not be actively looking to invest; they just have money sitting around and may be open to funding your deals if you ask them. Realize that a lot of people have money sitting in the bank earning literally less than 1 percent interest.

In fact, many of the lenders we have worked with over the years had no idea that they could invest their money this way. My uncle was a prime example of this. He had bought and sold real estate over the years, but had never lent private money. After I explained it to him, he became one of our lenders and has since loaned us money on a lot of our deals. My uncle and many of our lenders love lending because they earn points and interest on their money with the loans being secured by real estate.

Once you set up the relationship with a private money lender, you will find they will want to loan to you over and over again. Remember, they need you as much as you need them. Essentially, investing private money is the lender's opportunity to become a bank and reap the profits. There is no other investment vehicle like it.

FINDING EXISTING PRIVATE MONEY LENDERS

Anyone with money can become a private money lender. However, you need to know that in every city across the country there are already private money lenders actively making loans on properties that you can find. First, when someone makes a private money loan, the loan is recorded along with the name of the lender who made the loan. It takes work to track these lenders down, but when you do, it could be a great source of future funding for your business.

Another great way to find existing private money lenders is to network with other real estate professionals in your area who may have done business with a private money lender in the past. Ask your real estate agent, attorney, title agent, accountant, and other investors for contacts they know are loaning private money actively. A referral goes a long way, especially when you are working with a private money lender for the first time.

CAN YOU OPENLY ADVERTISE FOR PRIVATE MONEY LENDERS?

A private lending transaction can be considered a *security* under federal Securities and Exchange Commission (SEC) guidelines. Furthermore, since most states have securities regulations based on the federal SEC statutes, private lending for real estate investing can also be understood to be issuing a security under most state SEC regulations. In order to borrow money from private lenders, the investor must avoid making a public offering and say that the security is transacted *privately*. This way, the security can be transacted without registration. You should check with your state and understand the rules and exemptions that apply to you.

According to the SEC regulations, you cannot solicit for private lenders unless you're licensed to do so—therefore, you cannot technically advertise. This includes blind mailings, online and classified advertising, and so on. As a part of the SEC's criteria, you will need to have two or more substantial contacts with a potential lender prior to pitching any lending opportunity. So, it's important to make sure that you know the individual with whom you are speaking about private funding.

MEETING WITH THE LENDER FOR THE FIRST TIME

Once you have established contact with a lender you should set up a meeting at your office, the lender's office, or a coffee shop if you work out of your house. It is important that you take the time to answer any and all questions the lender has about private money lending and your company. Attached is a good outline to follow with important things to discuss when you are meeting with a potential private money lender.

Presentation Checklist for Private Lenders

❑ Research the lenders as much as possible to build rapport before talking to them.

❑ Ask them how their investments have been doing over the past 12 months.

❑ Ask them what their expectations are for the next 12 months that would satisfy them.

❑ Go over the company biography.

❑ Go over the business plan. (Explain how private lenders are protected through funding with documents.)

❑ Show them previous projects.

❑ Show them the subject property if you have one (full details, pictures, video, property packet).

❑ Discuss the social mission.

❑ Explain how they're protected with the equity position (tangible documents, comps, etc.).

❑ Explain the terms for this project (first lien/second lien, interest rate, etc.).

❑ Ask them how capitalized they are.

❑ Ask where the money is coming from.

❑ Ask how quickly they can fund.

❑ Ask how soon they can fund the next deal.

❑ Close or give them assignments to get a self-directed account set up.

CONCLUSION

Private money lenders can be great resource for your real estate business. Once they understand the nature of how a back-to-back wholesale transaction works it can become a great way for the lender to make money in a very short period of time. The lender will literally be wiring money to the title company or attorney, and then, a few days or a few months later, the lender gets his or her money back with points and interest. After you complete the first transaction with a new private money lender, he will literally want to become your new best friend. These private money relationships are very valuable and you can utilize their money for a wide variety of different types of real estate deals.

In the next chapter, we will look at two other really good sources of funding for your back-to-back closings: hard-money and transactional lenders.

CHAPTER 19

Working with Transactional Lenders and Hard-Money Lenders

The lack of money is the root of all evil.

—MARK TWAIN

One of my first wholesale deals was a vacant, boarded-up property in major disrepair. I ran the numbers and I knew it was a great deal. But there was a catch. The seller said that he would only sell me the property if I closed on it within two weeks.

When I put that property under contract, I knew I had to find a buyer—fast—and I did. But the investor who was interested in buying it from me had a problem: he didn't have enough cash of his own to purchase the property from me. I knew he wouldn't be able to get a traditional loan from a bank in time, not with this kind of closing timeframe.

So I scrambled. I did some digging, I pulled some strings, and I found a local hard-money lender who was willing to work with my buyer. That hard-money lender got the investor prequalified for the money he needed. One week later, the deal was fully funded. Obviously, I was impressed. And I ended up doing a lot of business with that hard-money lender over the years.

If your plan is to wholesale a lot of properties, then you definitely want to set up strong relationships with both transactional and hard-money lenders. Both of these types of lenders are *short-term lenders*. They're in the business of making loans to investors like the one who bought my deal—investors who purchase properties with the intention of flipping them for a profit.

A lot of hard-money lenders are also transactional lenders, and vice versa. In this chapter, I'll break down their differences, their similarities, and what you need to know about working with them.

WHAT IS TRANSACTIONAL FUNDING?

Many people confuse *transactional funding* with *hard-money loans*; however, there are a few main differences between the two. Both types of funding are extremely valuable and necessary for wholesalers who don't have the funds readily available to close deals quickly. However, while the terms of hard-money lending are quite strict, those of transactional lenders are less stringent.

Up until a few years ago, real estate investors often passed the financing through on their back-to-back closings, meaning investors would find a good deal, put it under contract, and open escrow for the A-B transaction. Then the investor would find another buyer who was willing to pay more for the property. The investor would then sign a second contract with the new buyer for a higher price and open a second escrow for the B-C transaction. Then the investor would use the C buyer's funding to fund the first A-B transaction. Then the investor would sell the property to the C buyer in the second B-C transaction. This was great, because the investor wholesaling the deal didn't have to bring any funds to close the deal and earned a profit in the middle.

However, when the real estate bubble burst, everything changed. There was intense scrutiny from lenders and title companies. A lot of title companies shied away from these types of transactions. Lenders also put stipulations in their underwriting guidelines to prevent this.

Most title companies are now requiring that the first closing be a standalone transaction where the investor funds the A-B purchase before the property can be resold to the C buyer. As a result, transactional funding became a big need for wholesalers.

Transactional funding is temporary funding for your acquisitions. It's a short-term loan that will allow you to secure the funds to purchase a property (A-B transaction), so you could immediately resell to a buyer. Appraisals, credit checks, and income verification are not always required because transactional funding is based on the wholesaler having a contract with the end-buyer already in place. That end C buyer is the person who will ultimately be the long-term owner of the property.

The transactional lender spends most of his time making sure that the C buyer has her funding in place and is ready to close the B-C transaction. Typically, the transactional lender funding your purchase won't release funds until your end C buyer has a clear to close, and the funds are sitting with the end buyer's title company or closing attorney.

Transactional funding is extremely short-term with loan lengths typically being 1–120 days, depending on the transaction. Some transactional lenders have *extended term* funding, which are loans for up to 60 days beyond the original time period in case the B-C transaction takes longer to close.

The fees for utilizing these funds will vary depending on how much money is required, the specific length of time the money is tied up, and the amount of risk entailed. Most transactional lender fees will charge two or three points (2–3% of the loan amount) and from 12 to 15 percent interest. Obviously, this will depend on the transactional lender's fee schedule, the deal, and what is negotiated.

Nevertheless, when a deal is profitable enough to offset the risk and the cost entailed in short-term loans, then having these transactional lenders on your real estate investing team is really important.

HARD-MONEY LENDING

In addition to finding a transactional lender you also want to set up a relationship with a hard-money lender. *Hard-money lenders* are lending companies that offer specialized short-term real estate–backed loans. The biggest difference between a transactional lender and a hard-money lender is the term length of the loan. A lot of hard-money lenders will loan money for at least six months and sometimes up to two or three years, depending on the real estate project.

Typically, hard money is used by rehabbers who are redeveloping properties and then flipping them a few months later. Hard-money lenders are companies who are licensed to lend money to investors and rehabbers buying homes in need of renovation. Hard-money lenders typically charge much higher interest rates because they fund deals that do not conform to bank standards such as verification of borrower's income, assets, or credit score.

Likewise, they will lend on properties that are in major need of repair that traditional lenders won't fund. In contrast to most traditional banks, hard-money lenders will generally also loan rehabbers the money they need for the construction.

This portion of funding is taken in *draws* against work being performed and renovation funds are usually set up on a payment schedule of work that has been completed. This is very similar to the payment schedule one would do for a contractor on a rehab project. Draws and payments are paid after work is completed.

WHEN YOU WILL USE A HARD-MONEY LENDER IN WHOLESALING

There are quite a few wholesaling scenarios where you may not be able to use a transactional lender and you will end up working with a hard-money lender.

First, some transactional lenders will only make loans for 30-day time periods. For example, if you are buying a short sale and the lender has a 90-day deed restriction, then you will not be able to use a transactional lender that will only loan money for 30 days. Thus, you will have to use a hard-money lender, which usually charges a higher interest rate and more points.

Second, you will want to refer a lot of your end C buyers to the hard-money lender you work with. This is invaluable because a lot of buyers may not be able to get conventional financing to buy the property from you, so you will have to refer them to a source where they can get funding.

KNOW THE TERMS

It's important that you know what the terms/criteria are when doing your research to see which lender fits your needs. Although all hard-money lenders lend on different terms, more often than not, they typically lend at a lower *loan-to-value* (LTV) ratio than a traditional bank. The LTV for a hard-money loan is calculated as loan value/ appraised value of the property, and is a measure of risk for lenders.

In most cases, hard-money lenders will only loan you up to 65–70 percent of the property's ARV (after-repaired value). This means that a hard-money lender can loan you up to 70 percent of what the home is worth in repaired condition.

Hard money does tend to be more expensive than many of the other sources of funding discussed in this book. This is mostly due to the heightened interest rates involved that cover the higher risk to the lender. They are not based upon traditional credit guidelines, which protect investors and banks from high default rates.

Hard-money lenders will typically charge a higher interest rate than traditional loans, anywhere between 12 and 18 percent, and usually between three and five points on the loan (1 point = 1% of the loan amount). Points are an additional fee charged based on the total loan amount. Some lenders will roll this fee into the loan. Hard-money loans are typically interest-only with a balloon payment of the principal balance due in six months to one year. Of course, these terms depend on how much money is put down, and how the loan is structured.

QUALIFYING FOR A HARD-MONEY LOAN

Each hard-money lender has its own borrower-qualification process. Hard-money lenders primarily determine their loans on the comparison of the property value *and* the purchase price. They would only lend up to a certain percentage of the ARV of the property. That way, if the borrower defaults on the loan, the lender would be able to foreclose, take over the property at a good enough discount, with equity still built in, where the lender can finish the renovations, sell the property, and profit handsomely.

Investors would get approved for a loan strictly based on the equity in the home, and not personal creditworthiness, making it extremely easy to qualify for a hard-money loan with less-than-perfect credit, a pending foreclosure, or income that is difficult to prove.

However, you will find that over the past few years, some hard-money lenders have become more strict on their terms to qualify for a loan. Some hard-money lenders now require more than just equity in the property to qualify if they want to stay in business.

This is because of changes in the economy and the new laws that are now favorable to borrowers. Consumer protection laws and expensive court procedures have forced some hard-money lenders to become even harsher, making it harder for some to qualify for a loan.

Of course, it's important to remember that all lenders are different and the specific criteria needed for approval depend on the lender. Some lenders in the real estate industry have moved toward requiring decent credit scores, W-2s and/or tax returns, your most recent pay stubs, bank statements, and down payments to reduce their risk, and some even ask for a personal guarantee on the loan as well.

It all boils down to the lender's assets being protected. However, there are still lenders in the market who only lend based on the property value itself, without all the additional qualifications that others now require. So you've got to make sure that you shop around to try to find the best lender for your business.

LOCATING HARD-MONEY AND TRANSACTIONAL LENDERS

There are two types of hard-money lenders you can work with: *national lenders* and *local lenders*. There are a very small number of national lenders that will lend in every state, so when first starting out, you will more than likely be working with local lenders.

Local lenders will often be the most flexible and offer more of a personal relationship. Both of these reasons will increase the probability of your borrowers getting approved. Contact them, introduce yourself, and explain that you will be sending them business. Ask them if they have any forms to expedite the approval process. Local lenders are looking for investors like you who will provide more than just one deal, so make sure to go out of your way to build a relationship with them.

CONCLUSION

As a wholesaler, the availability of money is more important than the cost of money. Transactional funding and hard-money lenders are essential for doing back-to-back closings when you don't have the necessary funds to carry them off yourself. You just have to calculate the cost of money into the profitability of the deal—and if it is still a highly profitable deal, then often it will make sense to borrow money even at higher interest rates.

After a few flips, you'll probably be able to start funding your back-to-back closings yourself. However, you will still want to refer a lot of your end buyers to your hard-money lenders for their funding needs, and in that respect these relationships will always be important.

In the next chapter, I'll show you how to build a trophy base of buyers so that you'll be able to move deals quickly with minimal stress.

CHAPTER 20

Building a Trophy Database of Buyers

Your trophy database is your most valuable asset. Build it, cultivate it, and treat it well.

—THAN MERRILL

One of the most critical facts about wholesaling is this: the larger your trophy database of buyers, the easier it becomes to wholesale properties. Nothing is more stressful than having someone accept your offer on her property, and then having to scramble around to find a buyer for it. That's why it is vital to start building a sizeable trophy database of potential buyers whom you can e-mail or call any time you have a wholesale deal for sale. Your trophy database of sellers, buyers, and contacts is the most valuable asset you have as a real estate investor.

You will interact with prospective buyers in a variety of ways from networking meetings to specific marketing campaigns you implement. Prospective buyers will respond to you via phone, e-mail, or in person. However you come across them, you must make sure you funnel them right into your trophy database. You will then want to continue marketing to these prospective buyers in order to build a relationship with them.

Over the next few chapters, I share several different strategies for building your buyers' list. Choose a few of these strategies to implement right away—even if you don't have a property for sale. Later, when you do put a property under contract, wholesaling your deal will be much easier as a result.

HOW YOU CAN LEVERAGE A DATABASE

In order for you see the bigger picture I am going to explain to you how we have built a trophy database, automated the relationship-building process, and communicate with our buyers over the course of time.

For example, there are a couple of real estate networking events I attend every month in my local area. At these networking groups I always meet at least two or three new prospective investor-buyers I have not met before. Whenever I meet new people, I make sure to get a business card from them or I write down their contact information if they don't have one.

When I get home I log into my online database and create a new "Investor-buyer" contact record. I then enter all of the buyer's information into the appropriate fields about this buyer. I also track how I met this person and make a note of when and where we met. Finally, if we talked about anything specific, I make a note about it in the contact record so I can remember the conversation later.

I then do two things after I create the contact record. First, from within my database I will send the buyer a personal e-mail just mentioning that I enjoyed meeting him the other day at the networking event. Second, I then drop that person into a 30-day e-mail auto-responder campaign where he will receive four prewritten e-mails from me over the course of the next month. This auto-responder campaign is specifically designed to build trust with the prospective buyer because each e-mail provides him with high-quality free information about buying investment properties.

When I do have a property I am going to wholesale I load up all the critical downloadable information about the deal for sale on my website. I will then send an e-mail, to either my entire buyers' list or a segment of my list, with a link to my website where they can view the property for sale.

If this prospective buyer calls about the property, I then gather more information about this buyer that I will transfer right into his contact record. This would include everything from the types of properties he is looking for, to the target areas he is looking at, to his financing capability. Over time, as I get to know the buyer better, the contact record matures because I inevitably have a lot of information about this person in his buyer record.

If I end up doing business with this buyer, I then tie this buyer record to the property I am selling and move them both through the various stages of the closing process within my database.

YOU MUST HAVE SOFTWARE TO BUILD A TROPHY DATABASE

Obviously, this is a much better system than having a bunch of business cards stacked up on your desk or in a shoebox in one of your drawers. This is not a Daytimer, Outlook, or Gmail, either, because they aren't specific enough to the real estate business.

As your database grows, you're going to want to add to the initial information you collected from the prospective buyers beyond just their name, phone, address, and e-mail. I call this *maturing the contact record* within a database because you will add what areas they are targeting, what their financing is like, as well as the names of spouses and kids, birthdates, and special interests. This information will be vital to selling properties as well as building referral business.

The database I use is a complete all-in-one real estate business management system. It is a Client Relationship Management (CRM) system that has marketing automation tools built right into it. I use this software to manage all of my marketing, all the deals I am working on, and all of my contacts. There are also real estate–specific tools built right into the software.

If you are interested in seeing a demo of how this database works, go to www .FortuneBuilders.com for more information.

CONCLUSION

Don't wait until you have a property under contract to build a buyers' list and a trophy database. This should be an activity that you focus on every week. Eventually, you will develop a core group of serious buyers with whom you will work over and over again. Until then, look at everyone as a prospective buyer, and seize every chance you can to add them to your buyers' list.

When you focus on building your trophy database, you'll start to reach a wider audience of people, and your business will begin to expand. The next chapter will show you how to network to find buyers you can add to your trophy database.

Coaching Student Success Story

FIGURE 20.1   Coaching Students Wes & Sheela
Reproduced by permission of Wes Dorsey.

Coaching Students' Names: Wes and Sheela Dorsey
Property Location: Garland, Texas
Purchase Price: $64,000
Transaction Costs: $3,124
Sale Price: $74,000
Profit: $6,876

Student Story: Wes and Sheela were investing on a part-time basis when they started coaching with us. With our help and their determination they are now both full-time investors. The flexibility of working in real estate has enabled them to spend more time with their children while creating a very comfortable lifestyle.

Deal Summary: The seller of this property reached out to Wes and Sheela through Facebook. The seller living in the property could not keep up with the maintenance on the property and it was becoming a money pit. The seller had fallen behind on the mortgage and did not have the financial capability to make the necessary repairs that the property needed.

FIGURE 20.2   Real Estate Deal in Garland, TX
Reproduced by permission of Wes Dorsey.

Wes and Sheela offered to purchase the property for $64,000, which paid off the mortgage and gave the seller enough money to find a more affordable place to live.

Wes and Sheela then marketed the property to their existing buyers' list they had already started building. They sent out a packet of information about the property to their buyers' list and found a buyer for the property at $74,000. Having already developed a list of buyers was critical to their success on this particular deal.

For more information about our coaching go to: www.FortuneBuildersMastery .com.

CHAPTER 21

Networking to Find Buyers

Be more concerned about making others feel good about themselves than you are making them feel good about you.

—DAN REILAND

Literally anyone you meet can be a buyer or a referral source. That's why, as a wholesaler, you need to get the word out about what you do. That's why, if you're shy, you need to push yourself beyond the limits of your comfort zone now and then. That's why it's critical to network.

As a wholesaler, it is absolutely vital that you build solid relationships with other investors and real estate professionals in your area. Networking is a key way to start building your trophy database of buyers—and to start generating referral business.

In most areas, there's no shortage of networking groups and meetings. It won't cost you a lot of money to attend these meetings. What it will cost you is time. But in this case, you have to make the time if you want to network effectively.

In this chapter, I teach you where to find a lot of other investors hanging out in one place so that you can network strategically. I also discuss the various types of real estate professionals you will want to build relationships with in order to boost referrals for your business.

STRATEGIC NETWORKING OPPORTUNITIES

Auctions

In most cases, you'll find your most serious investor-buyers at local property auctions. There are many different types of auctions and you can usually find local foreclosure auctions happening in your area on a daily or weekly basis. You can also network with buyers at *tax deed auctions*, which are held by the local state government. At these auctions, properties sold will have back delinquent taxes owed.

Similar to the foreclosure auction, buyers can only purchase these properties with cash. These can be some of the best individuals to have on your buyers' list, because you know they can close quickly. There are also private auction companies you can find online that many times will hold private auctions in certain select cities around the country.

The great thing about auctions is that most require that winning bidders close on the property in a very short period of time. This means the majority of investors who are bidding will most likely close on the property in cash. This will, of course, depend on the type of auction and the state in which you live.

Whenever you go to an auction try to meet as many people as you can and gather as many business cards as you can and add them to your buyers' list. Most investors will be very receptive to anyone who might have a good wholesale deal for sale now or in the future. As always, tell them who you are and what you do upfront, and also let them know that you are constantly finding amazing deals in the area. Make a point of telling them that you would be more than happy to share the wealth by contacting them the next time you have a property of their interest.

If you are looking to sell a property right away, this is one of the first places to go because inevitably you will meet some very serious buyers who have bought properties in the past. If you have to close on your wholesale deal very quickly, then you only want to work with experienced buyers who have the ability to close with cash.

Local REIA and Landlord Association Meetings

Real Estate Investor Association (REIA) meetings and Landlord Association meetings are a good place to network with other real estate investors and real estate professionals in your market. You will find a wide variety of experience levels at these networking meetings; however, most clubs have a very large percentage of new investors. Likewise, some of these groups are very well run and others are not. It all depends on who is running the club, their organizational skills, and how well they market.

Not every city has a local real estate investing or landlord group, but most major cities do. If there is one in your local area, you should be able to find it fairly easily online. You can also ask other investors, real estate agents, or mortgage professionals for information about the clubs in your local area. If one doesn't exist, you might consider starting one.

Some of these clubs are free, but most charge monthly or annual fees to help support the club. If you're just starting out as an investor, your goal should be to attend these club meetings at least once a month, network efficiently, and get your name out there in the local market. Depending on the size of the club you may even consider becoming a vendor or a sponsor.

At the meetings you should make it a goal to meet as many people as possible. You also want to identify who some of the more experienced investors are. Build rapport with them and find out as much information as possible about their business and what types of properties they prefer.

Chamber of Commerce and Business Networking Groups

I highly recommend attending one of your upcoming Chamber of Commerce events. These present great opportunities to meet other business owners and working professionals in your area. I personally have sold a lot of properties to people I met at a local Chamber of Commerce event. This is also a great place to meet private lenders who could fund transactions for you.

Depending on where you live there may be other various business networking groups who get together on a monthly basis. You can usually find these groups on www.MeetUp.com or on a local community website.

Home/Trade Shows

Home shows and trade shows are places where you generally find a lot of real estate professionals, contractors, lenders, and building suppliers. These are great places to go to network with other people in the real estate business. You might even consider getting a booth because a lot of these trade shows will see a few thousand people over the course of a few days.

Social Media

Social media is a great way to network and build relationships with investors who live in your area. Facebook, Twitter, LinkedIn, Pinterest, and Instagram are all great social media sites you can join where you will find groups of investors hanging out. You will find online groups that have formed on these sites where real estate investors hang out and network with each other. You can also message investors individually on these platforms and connect on a more personal level.

While each network is powerful on its own, today most people connect through a multitude of social media sites using hyperlinks and #hashtags.

Hosting Your Own Events

A great way to educate your marketplace and build your wholesale buyers' list is by hosting educational/networking events yourself. Over the years we have done this and it has proven to be very effective. We have also done this in a variety of different ways.

For example, we frequently present to entire offices of Realtors on various educational topics. In fact, a lot of brokers bring in local vendors and real estate professionals to provide continuing education to their agents. We frequently speak to offices about "how to negotiate short sales" and "how to work with real estate investors." These educational topics have proven to be a great source of referrals for us over the years.

We have also occasionally held free educational events at the properties we are rehabbing. We call these "rehab subgroups" and they attract a lot of other investors in the area who want to learn how to rehab and make money flipping properties. We advertise these meetings to our buyers' list and through social media.

Over the years we have added a lot of people to our buyers' list through these meetings and sold a lot of properties because of them. It is a great way of positioning yourself and building trust with people who do business in your area. When you share your knowledge, your resources, and your experiences it *always* benefits your business in ways you never expected. It's called the *law of reciprocation*.

NETWORKING WITH OTHER REAL ESTATE PROFESSIONALS

Meeting with other professionals in the real estate industry will inevitably help your business in two ways. These professionals can refer you both deals you might want to buy and buyers for the deals that you do find.

Always keep in mind that whatever you need, someone else already has it. You just have to build relationships with those individuals and get them to remember you when they come across one of these opportunities. You never know when a strategic business relationship will lead you to a transaction that earns you a profit.

Let's discuss a few key real estate professionals you will want to network and build relationships with.

Hard-Money Lenders

Hard-money lenders are some of the best people to build relationships with—not only to borrow money from, but also because they can refer you a lot of buyers for your wholesale deals. Hard-money lenders are in the business of loaning money to investors who rehab and redevelop properties. They inevitably work with and know many of the larger investors in the area because they lend money to them. They are also always qualifying new borrowers whom they will lend to in the future.

Over the years, I have sold a lot of properties to investors whom I first met through local hard-money lender introductions. These relationships have proven to be very valuable for me.

Additionally, you will want to refer many of the other investors you meet in other ways to your hard-money lender contacts so they can get qualified for financing. You will find a lot of investors who are interested in your properties, but don't have the capital necessary to buy from you. You will also be able to help more serious buyers buy multiple properties from you when you set them up with a good hard-money lender. It really is a two-way street that can benefit your wholesaling business immensely.

If you build a really strong relationship with a hard-money lender who has built a trophy database of investors, you might even be able to convince the lender to send an e-mail out about one of your wholesale deals for sale.

Other Wholesalers

Inevitably, there are other people who live in your area who wholesale properties. I highly recommend you build relationships with them for two reasons. First, they may have great deals you might consider buying yourself. Second, more experienced wholesalers usually have a buyers' list they have built over the years.

If you develop a relationship with them, you might consider entering into a joint venture on the deal if they feel they have an investor they know would be willing to purchase the deal. Other wholesalers can also help with financing if you are going to be double closing on the property.

Real Estate Agents

Real estate agents are a great source of buyer referrals. Obviously, they are in the business of putting together sellers and buyers and the good ones have built trophy databases themselves. Please understand there are probably a lot of Realtors in your area, so you will want to be strategic with your time by networking with the ones who are more experienced and who list and sell a lot of houses on an annual basis.

One of the first things I did in my area was use the Multiple Listing Service (MLS) to find out who the top 20 Realtors were. In most, but not all, areas the MLS allows you to search and find who the top sellers' and buyers' agents are, based on the number of closed transactions. You will have to find a savvy agent who knows how to run this report within the MLS. Once you have a list of those Realtors, reach out to each one of them to build a relationship. Realize these top agents already have clients they work with so you have to get their attention and make sure they take you seriously.

I made it a point to take every one of them in my area to lunch or for coffee. Not every meeting has led to a closed deal, but over the years I have built some very profitable relationships from these meetings.

When you do make contact with these top Realtors you want to find out what types of properties and areas they specialize in. Most Realtors work a geographic area and prefer to work with certain types of properties.

Be aware that when a Realtor brings you a potential buyer she will most likely be representing that buyer in the transaction. Thus, you will have a commission that needs to be factored into the deal.

Mortgage Brokers

Mortgage brokers can also be a good source of buyer referrals. They will refer you both investor buyers and retail buyers. Ideally, you get to know the owner of one of the local mortgage companies who has a large number of mortgage brokers who work for him. This is a great relationship because the owner can let all the brokers know about your business and what types of properties you sell. The most successful mortgage brokers also build trophy databases of clients they have worked with over the years. If you build a really good relationship, they might even consider sending an e-mail to their client list about the property you are selling.

Contractors

A lot of contractors work with investors who buy investment properties. So always be conscious to ask contractors for referrals when you meet with them or work with them. Also, remember contractors are great buyers themselves. A lot of contractors want to get into flipping houses; however, most don't know how to find the deals. Over the years we have sold a lot a properties to the contractors who work with us. We have found contractors to be great buyers because they are very confident in their construction knowledge and can save money by working on the house themselves as opposed to hiring out the work. You will definitely want to connect contractors with sources of financing like your hard-money lender in case they don't have the funding available to purchase your property.

Section 8

In some areas, the government housing agency compiles a list of property owners who participate in Section 8 housing. Take a trip down to the Section 8 housing office and ask if they have a list of every landlord who participates in Section 8 housing in the area and if it is available to the public.

Property Management Companies

Property management companies manage properties for real estate investors. If you get to know a few of the larger property managers in your area, they can refer you to investors who are looking for real estate deals. Generally, their clients prefer apartment buildings and commercial properties so they can be a great source if you are looking to wholesale a commercial property.

Since they manage other investors' properties, they are usually the first to know which investors are looking to sell or buy new properties. Most of the time, however, these property managers also invest in their own property and, as a result, they are always on the lookout for new deals.

HOW TO BUILD RELATIONSHIPS AND STAND OUT FROM THE CROWD

Remember, building your buyers' list through networking takes patience, skill, and follow-through. Getting someone to trust you is not easy and takes time and a process for doing so. I have always consciously asked people I meet two really important questions that have helped me immensely:

Question 1: "What is the most important project you are working on right now in your personal or professional life?"

Question 2: "Is there any way I, or someone in my network, can help you with that?"

I have found these two questions to be the key to building successful business relationships. So many people who network focus only on themselves and how people can benefit them. If you first focus on how you can be of service to someone else, then they are much more likely to do business with you long term. Often, a simple follow-up e-mail and putting someone I just met in contact with someone else who can help her with something is how I get my foot in the door to some very valuable business relationships.

This is why building a trophy database of buyers is so important. As you meet, classify, and build relationships with people in your area you can leverage those relationships and put people in contact with each other. That "relationship currency" is of tremendous value to you and something that will provide dividends to you down the road.

CONCLUSION

Networking well will move you one step closer to developing that key handful of buyers who trust you and who will purchase properties from you frequently. In the meantime, refer to rule #1: anyone you meet can end up being a referral source for your business. Always continue to add new contacts to your buyers' list as you network.

Another way to find buyers is through direct response marketing campaigns. We look at these campaigns and how to utilize them to find even more potential buyers in the next chapter.

CHAPTER 22

Direct Response Marketing Strategies to Find Buyers

Marketing is a contest for people's attention.

—Seth Godin

The secret to longevity in the real estate investing business is to become a marketing rainmaker. You've already learned the power of utilizing direct response marketing campaigns to find motivated sellers. However, direct response marketing is just as effective at the other end of the transaction as well.

The immutable law of marketing declares that there is a direct relationship between the number of prospects you have and the income you earn. No matter how much you know about the business, how hard you work at being better than your competition, or how much you try to be different and stand out from the crowd, at the end of the day what matters most is how many leads you generate. If you don't have leads, you don't have a sustainable long-term business.

Direct response marketing is a technique designed to generate a direct response from a potential customer by making an appealing offer, often in the form of a free premium for responding. Direct response marketing is also the polar opposite of *branding* or *image marketing*, which focuses on the advertiser and not the customer. Anyone who is championing that they are number one or the best in an area is not focusing on the customer. They are focusing on themselves.

The ways we market to buyers through direct response marketing are very similar to the methods we use when we market to sellers. The difference is in the messages we use to get them to respond.

Your goal is to build a buyers' list by getting a lot of people to respond to your campaign. You will market your wholesale deals to that list now and in the future.

I have found that many real estate investors make the mistake of waiting too long to begin their direct response marketing campaigns to find buyers. The problem is that if you find a good deal and the seller wants you to close quickly, you may not have time to find a buyer. This is why it is so important to start executing direct response marketing campaigns for buyers at the same time you're marketing to find deals to purchase.

In this chapter, I am going to take you through some of the most strategic direct response marketing campaigns that we have used over the years and show you how to put them into practice yourself.

CRAIGSLIST, BACKPAGE, AND OTHER ONLINE-CLASSIFIED-AD WEBSITES

Placing ads on Craigslist, Backpage, and other online-classified websites is a very effective way to build a buyers' list. These websites attract a lot of eyeballs on a daily basis and are a great way to build a buyers' list. Most of these sites are free, although some charge a small fee.

On Craigslist, for example, you can place ads in the housing section under "Real Estate for Sale." There is no shortage of creative ways to get people to click on one of your ads. What is most important is that you offer something of value to a potential investor.

Some Good Craigslist Advertising Headlines

- "Looking to buy a house under market value?"
- "Investors wanted! Cheap houses available!"
- "Free Foreclosure List—Discounted Properties Available"
- "This house is a *great* deal! I have others, too . . ."
- "Great real estate deals for sale! Look inside . . ."
- "Investor special—must sell!"
- "Cash investors wanted! Discounted homes available"

The key is to get your headline to stand out among all the other properties that are currently listed for sale by other brokers and Realtors. Once again, when people click on your advertisement it is best to give them multiple reasons to go visit your website and opt in to join your buyers' list.

You don't have to have a property to advertise to place an advertisement on Craigslist. Just give investors a few compelling reasons to call you or to opt in on one of your websites.

The great thing about Craigslist is that it's free, so you can always switch up the wording in your ads to see what works and what doesn't. Keep in mind that ads can be hit-or-miss because they can get pushed down pretty easily depending on the number of new ads being placed that day. Don't get discouraged if you post an ad and don't get any responses. If you are consistent and make a habit of posting one or two ads daily, you will start getting calls and people opting into your website. I also suggest training an assistant or a virtual assistant to do this for you.

Finally, you can also contact other investors selling properties who are listing their properties on Craigslist. Inevitably, you will find a lot of investors using the resource to market their properties for sale, so don't be afraid to reply to their advertisements and pick up the phone and call them about any deal you are selling.

FACEBOOK REAL ESTATE GROUPS

Social networking sites like Facebook are extremely useful ways to build a buyers' list and connect with other investors. First, you should spend some time searching for local Facebook real estate investor groups in your area. Become a member of the group and add value to it.

Then occasionally post and give people a good reason to join your buyers' list. Ideally, you let them know that you have investment deals for sale, and when they opt into your buyers' list you e-mail them when you have your next deal for sale. You can also send private messages to members of the group and connect with them on an individual basis.

COMPANY WEBSITE

As an investor, it's extremely important to have a company website for credibility purposes and to have a place where people can opt in to join your buyers' list. On your company websites you can showcase your properties for sale and for rent, but you should also try to generate leads from the site itself by making sure people can opt in right on your website to your buyers' list. There are many resources available where you can get affordable website solutions. If you would like to see what we use, visit www.FortuneBuilders.com.

LEAD-GENERATION PAGES (SQUEEZE PAGES)

Squeeze pages are single-action websites. This type of website has only one purpose: to get visitors to fill out a form on the site so they can be added to your buyers' list. When someone opts in on either our company website or one of our squeeze pages he or she is automatically added to our trophy database as a new buyer record. The less information you ask for, the better the page will convert. We usually want people's name, phone, and e-mail address only. That way we can get in contact with them in the future in one of two ways.

On your squeeze page you should test different free offers or reasons why someone should join your buyers' list beyond just getting access to discounted properties. Offer something of value to the visitor such as a free report on "How to Find Cheap Properties" or a "Free Local Foreclosure List" and you will get a higher conversion rate.

PENNY SAVER NEWSPAPERS

A lot of areas have a *Penny Saver* newspaper or a small local paper that you can place advertisements in. The cost will vary based on the newspaper's distribution and the paper itself. You should also look for other investors who are advertising in the newspaper and call them and add them to your buyers' list.

REACHING OUT TO YOUR COMPETITION

One of the most time-consuming but best ways to add other investors to your buyers' list is to pick up the phone and call them from the advertisements they place. In every city you will inevitably run across competitors who advertise to buy real estate.

Any time you see your competitors' advertisements you should do two things: put their name, phone number, and any other information you have into your trophy database. You should then pick up the phone and call them and introduce yourself. If you make a connection, get their e-mail address and make sure they know that any time you have a future deal for sale you will send an e-mail about the property with the details.

Here are a few places you will find advertisements placed by other investors:

- Craigslist
- Backpage

- Facebook
- LinkedIn
- Pay-per-click ads
- Bandit signs
- Billboards
- Bus benches
- Radio
- TV
- Newspaper ads
- "Property for Sale" signs
- "Property for Rent" signs

Remember, you can't just scrape e-mails from any online site and start e-mailing them without their permission. That's why you should only reach out to them if they are advertising something for sale and make sure you get their permission to contact them after that.

When potential buyers contact you, make sure to add them to your buyers' list and give them a call the next time you have something that fits their criteria. However, if you plan to use bandit signs to market for buyers, remember to check your local ordinances, as some areas have restrictions on where signs can and cannot be placed.

CASH BUYERS

You might be shocked at how many people in your area are buying properties with all cash. Last year, California alone reported that slightly less than a third of all property sales were to cash buyers. Cash buyers are the best buyers to work with because the transactions go so much more smoothly. This is why you definitely want to find and market to cash buyers in your area if you are going to be wholesaling properties.

Whenever a property is sold in your area it is a transaction that becomes part of the public record. If there is no mortgage or lender with a lien against the property, then the buyer most likely purchased the property in cash. Thus, you can find cash buyers by trolling through the public records. It is a time-consuming process, which is why I highly recommend you buy a "cash buyer" list from a list broker rather than putting the data together yourself.

CONCLUSION

These are just a few of the better strategies to find other investors in your area through direct response marketing. Start by implementing one of them right away to begin building your trophy database of buyers. As your database grows, track how many new buyers you are adding each week. Monitoring growth is a key part of building a successful wholesaling business.

Beyond marketing to buyers, you can also find business by marketing your wholesale deals themselves. I'll cover all the bases of how to do that in the next chapter.

Coaching Student Success Story

FIGURE 22.1　Coaching Student Clint Jones
Reproduced by permission of Clint Jones.

Coaching Student's Name: Clint Jones
Property Location: Tulsa, Oklahoma
Purchase Price: $224,500
Transaction Costs: $15,800
Gross Profit: $51,200

Deal Summary: Clint found this large, 5,100-square-foot property in his neighborhood that was scheduled to go to auction a few weeks later. On the Saturday of the auction he was surprised to see only six people register to bid on the property. The next thing he knew, he was the winning bidder and still $15,000 under the maximum allowable offer he calculated based on the after-repair value and estimated repair cost.

He had 30 days to close on the property at his winning bid of $224,500. He immediately marketed the home on Craigslist and found a buyer three days before he had to close. Because the buyer was getting bank financing, Clint knew he would have to close on the property using hard money and then resell the

FIGURE 22.2   Real Estate Deal in Tulsa, OK
Reproduced by permission of Clint Jones.

property after the buyer got his bank financing in line. The buyer had to ultimately go through a few lenders to get financing. As a result, Clint ended up negotiating a sale price of $280,000, plus he had the buyer cover $10,000 of his transaction and holding costs.

Clint ended up making a profit of $51,200 on the wholesale deal.

For more information about our coaching go to: www.FortuneBuildersMastery.com.

Marketing Your Wholesale Deal

I was a pretty good coach and working with marketing was like coaching.

—Bernard Ebbers

To sell a wholesale property, you need to do three things. First, you need to provide your potential buyers with critical information, both to get them interested in the deal and to inspire them to make a quick decision. Second, you need to make sure that the people who are on your buyers' list know about the property you have for sale. And finally, you need to market the deal to the general public.

As a wholesaler, you will always be using your trophy database of buyers to sell your deals. But that doesn't mean it's safe to put all your eggs in one basket. When you get a property under contract, you also need a plan to market it properly to the general public. The more you market your deals, the more your buyers' list will grow.

MAKE SURE YOUR TROPHY DATABASE IS ORGANIZED

As you add people to your buyers' list inside your trophy database you want to make sure you collect as much contact information as possible, so when you have a deal for sale you can let them know about it in various ways. You want to always make sure your trophy database is organized. This means you should be constantly cleaning and updating the data inside your database. For example, if you have a lot of old e-mail addresses, you want to make sure you purge them from your database because when you send mass e-mails this could hurt your e-mail deliverability rate to the valid e-mail addresses within your database.

ASSEMBLE THE CRITICAL INFORMATION INTO A WHOLESALE DEAL MARKETING PACKAGE

You want to make it very easy for buyers to make a decision about the property you are looking to wholesale. Thus, you should give them all the critical information they need to make a decision without overwhelming them. The goal is to get them to make a very quick decision because you are under a timeline to sell the property. Here is the critical information you will want to assemble about the deal and put together into a "Wholesale Deal Marketing Package." You can then put this PDF up on your website along with any pictures you took of the property for people to download.

Here is what should go inside your Wholesale Deal Marketing Package:

- *Terms of the deal:* I let them know the address of the property, the sale price, the estimated repair cost, and the after-repair value of the property. I also let the buyers know when they would have to close by, and exactly what types of offers I will be considering.
- *Property card:* A property card is a PDF of the tax assessor's field card that has details about the property.
- *Pictures or video of the property:* Ideally, you have a lot of pictures and or video of the property you are looking to wholesale. I prefer to include at least 15 to 20 pictures of the property so buyers can get a very good feel for what type of work needs to be done.
- *Repair list:* I include a list of repairs that the property needs. I usually just give the buyer a PDF copy of the repair list I made when I analyzed the property to buy.
- *Sold comparables:* I include at least three sold comparables of properties that are good after repair-value comparables. Make sure these are traditional sales and that there are plenty of pictures of these properties included with the comparables.

CALL YOUR MOST SERIOUS BUYERS FIRST

Whenever you get a property under contract you will want to call your most serious buyers first. How many people you will actually call about the deal will depend, but start with at least 5 to 10 buyers you know have the ability to make an all-cash offer.

Over time, you will find that you will be selling to the same people over and over again. We sell the majority of our properties with a few phone calls today. However, it wasn't always this way, which is why I discuss other ways to let people know about your wholesale property for sale.

E-MAIL BLASTS

The second thing you want to do after you call a few of your most serious investor-buyers is send an e-mail to your entire buyers' list. This is a great way to reach a large audience in a very short period of time. Ideally, you should drive them to your website with all of the pertinent information about the deal for sale.

The key to success with e-mail marketing is to be creative and get your e-mails opened. Remember, most people won't open your e-mail when you send it, so you have to have a very catchy headline. Your e-mails must stand out among the myriad e-mails that your buyers receive on a daily basis.

Here are some subject lines I have used that had great open rates:

- "Don't let the grass scare you. This deal is *weediculous!*"
- "Honey, stop the car—this deal is awesome!"
- "My wife comes with this house . . ."
- "Ugly houses need love, too!"
- "This house is a *moneymaker!*"

Write a short description about the property that also ties into the subject line of your e-mail. Your description should also focus on the highlights of the deal and get your recipients to visit your website to download the Wholesale Deal Marketing Package. Of course, you can always have them call you or e-mail you directly as well, and then you can e-mail them the information after you speak to them.

Finally, you should send a follow-up e-mail to your buyers' list if you find a buyer for the property quickly. This will create a sense of urgency among some of your buyers the next time you market a property for sale via e-mail.

TEXT BLASTING

Mobile marketing strategies such as text messaging can help you reach your buyers on a more personal level than e-mail and they generally get much higher open rates. You will probably find that your e-mail open rates are typically less than 20 percent when you e-mail people a couple of times a month.

A text message, on the other hand, often gets read. Studies have shown that texts are usually read by 80-percent-plus of the people who receive them. And they typically get read faster than when you send an e-mail. Within 15 minutes of sending a text blast, most of the people you sent it to will have read the message.

Think to yourself: Every time your mobile phone beeps or vibrates, how long does it take you to read the text message? This form of marketing is best when you want an instant response.

Here are some key points to remember when doing text message marketing:

- The messages have to be concise and you must include a way for people to opt out from receiving future text messages.
- Drive people to your website if you have the details of the property for sale listed there. Otherwise, have them call you back directly.
- Make sure your phone number and website links are working before you send the text blast out.
- Remove anyone from your text blast service who asks not to be contacted again.

VOICE BROADCASTING

Voice broadcasting (voice blasts) is yet another way to get in touch with your buyers' list without spending a great deal of time calling each person individually. This is a mass-communication technique that allows you to send hundreds or thousands of pre-recorded messages to your buyers' list. Only a certain percentage of people will open your e-mail so this is a great way of making sure that a higher percentage of your buyers' list knows you have a property you're looking to wholesale. Here is an example of a message you can use:

Hi, this is (Your Name) from (Your Company Name) and I wanted to let you know about a great real estate investment opportunity I have under contract in (City Name). You can visit my website at (www.YourWebsiteHere) and get all the details about the deal. I will be showing the property over the next few days. If you are interested, call me back at (Your Phone Number). This is a great opportunity you do not want to miss out on.

There are numerous voice broadcast services you can use that have great features that you can find online very easily. A voice blast works great in tandem with an e-mail and you should send both on the same day to maximize effectiveness.

WHAT IF YOU HAVE A DEAL TO SELL BUT DON'T HAVE A BUYERS' LIST?

If you haven't yet built a buyers' list, then you will want to refer back to Chapters 20, 21, and 22 on how to build a buyers' list. All of those marketing resources and campaigns mentioned in those chapters are also very effective for marketing your individual wholesale deals to the general public.

CONCLUSION

You don't have time to waste when you're wholesaling. That's why you need to give your buyers exactly what they need to make a financial evaluation on your properties quickly. It's also why you need to have a solid methodology in place for working smoothly with your buyers.

In the next chapter, I give you some strategies on how to classify, prescreen, and communicate with the buyers who contact you about your wholesale deals for sale.

Classifying, Prescreening, and Communicating with Buyers

A satisfied customer is the best business strategy of all.

—Michael LeBoeuf

In the real estate game, you are constantly juggling one all-important asset: *time*.

When I first got started in real estate, I wasted boatloads of time. I met with anybody and everybody. Someone called me up, and I'd be so excited that I'd get in my car and head off to go talk to them. I spent 40 or 50 hours a month meeting buyers who had no intention of making an offer on my properties. Worse, at least five or six deals fell apart that first year just because I didn't know how to properly prescreen and vet buyers.

It was a colossal waste of my most important resource. But I learned something critical from the experience, and that was the importance of creating a systemized process to classify, prescreen, and communicate with potential buyers.

While you are building your buyers' list, you must be able to execute all of these things. This chapter will give you the strategies you need to deal efficiently with buyers.

CLASSIFY BUYERS WITHIN YOUR TROPHY DATABASE

Once you have a buyers' list within your trophy database you are going to want to start organizing and segmenting it. An unorganized database can be a huge time suck for you. When you spend all of your time and energy on the wrong buyers, you'll end up losing a lot of precious time that you will never get back.

Ideally you only want to market properties to buyers who are interested in those types of properties. Unfortunately, the majority of the time, you won't know who your buyers are, especially if they initially found you and opted in on one of your websites. Thus, you will have a *main* list of uncategorized buyers and smaller *sub-lists* of buyers you have placed there because you found out exactly what types of properties they are interested in. Your goal is to move people from your main list to a specific category as you get to know them better.

Here are the five categories you should use:

1. *Main list:* This is where everyone will go when you first meet them or when they opt in online.
2. *Retail buyers:* Retail buyers are end-users who plan on moving into the property. They usually only buy once every five to seven years and typically will pay the most for properties. They have very specific wants and desires.
3. *Lease option buyers:* These are renters who want to buy a property, but they either don't have the credit or don't have the finances to buy a property from you. However, they would be interested in possible rent-to-own opportunities.
4. *Rehabber buyers:* These are investor-buyers interested in fixing and flipping properties that you wholesale.
5. *Landlord buyers:* These are investor-buyers interested in owning properties they will rent and earn cash flow from.

Generally speaking, you will find that about 5 percent of your list will close on 80 percent of your deals. You need to get to know this 5 percent better and send them deals that meet their criteria. These are the individuals you will also want to call the next time you have a deal for sale before you end up marketing it to your entire buyers' list.

THE IMPORTANCE OF PRESCREENING BUYERS

Many beginning investors meet with every prospective buyer they come in contact with and spend much of their time talking about would-be deals to would-be buyers. There are a lot of new buyers out there who will sign a contract to purchase a wholesale deal from you, but their inexperience often can slow down the closing and make the transaction more laborious. You don't want to risk ruining your reputation because you didn't take the time to prescreen potential buyers properly. *Prescreening* is a very important step in the wholesale process, but you need to make it more time efficient by creating a systemized process to prescreen your buyers.

Sometimes, when you first meet wholesale buyers, they may have recently bought a property (or may have multiple properties they have recently received financing for) and, therefore, they may have leveraged all the funds they have access to at the present time. However, two months later, they may have the necessary cash at their disposal again to finance their next property. That's why, when you meet buyers, it's best to update their buyer contact record in your trophy database so you can sell a property to them in the future.

WHAT TO DO WHEN BUYERS CONTACT YOU

The first time you are prescreening prospective buyers, you want to gather as much information as possible. This assures that you don't waste your valuable time on buyers who are not absolutely serious or who don't have sufficient means to close on a transaction. I prefer to prescreen buyers right over the phone when they call me about one of my wholesale deals for sale.

I use a script to make sure I gather all the pertinent information before I show the buyer the property. I then save that script as a PDF inside my trophy database attached to the buyer's contact record. I will then update the buyer's contact record with all the information the person provided me over the phone.

WHAT YOU NEED TO KNOW ABOUT A BUYER

First, you want to know the experience level of the person you are talking to on the phone. It's easier to build rapport with someone when you know a little bit about the person's experience level. The last thing you want to do is talk down to a serious buyer or talk over the head of a newbie. So I always ask the following three questions to make sure I get a feel for the person's experience level:

1. "Have you been investing for a while, or are you just getting started?"
2. "What types of properties are you looking for specifically?"
3. "Are you working on other properties right now?"

Second, you want to see if the buyer has reviewed all of the information you sent out about the deal in your Wholesale Deal Marketing Package. If not, you will have to explain the terms of the deal to the buyer.

Third, you want to know how the buyer would plan on financing the property if he or she did decide to put in an offer. Cash buyers are the easiest to work with so I want to know if they have the means to close on the property in cash. If they don't, I usually recommend they get in contact with one of my hard-money lender contacts I have worked with before. If they don't have the funding available to buy the property, then I will not show them the property until I know that they spoke with my hard-money lender and funding looks like a possibility.

COMMUNICATING PROPERLY AND TRAINING YOUR WHOLESALE BUYERS

Finally, before you ever show potential buyers the property you want to make sure they understand the nature of the transaction. Here is exactly what I tell all the buyers I speak to over the phone:

> Before I show you the property, I want to make sure you understand the nature of this deal. I currently have this property under contract, which means I have an equitable interest in the property, but I do not currently own the property. I have a purchase contract with the seller that I am looking to sell. I am prepared to close on the property, and in certain situations I will. However, that will depend on the buyer I am working with and how they plan on financing the property. It is important to know that I have a set closing date with the seller and any buyer I work with would have to close on or before that date. Likewise, there will be other investors looking at this property and I will look at all offers that come in. I would guess that many of these offers will be "all cash" and will have no inspection contingencies, or, if they do, very short ones. If you are working with a lender, I will have to make sure they also understand the nature of the transaction so it does not get hung up in underwriting. I will most likely be making a decision on this property within the next few days, so I encourage you to act quickly.

It is important for you to be completely transparent about the nature of the transaction with any buyer or agent you are talking to. Do not hide anything because that is the quickest way to have a transaction blow up in your face.

Finally, I will set up a time to show the buyer the property if I feel the person is serious. If not, I will tell the buyer to drive by the property and call me back if he or she is still interested in setting up a time to see it.

CONCLUSION

All decisions are helped by momentum, and opportunities to make money do not last long. Make that point clear to every one of your potential buyers. Let your buyers know that you have had positive experiences in wholesaling, and explain to them how you have made money doing the same thing they are about to do. When you know how to classify, screen for, and communicate with quality buyers, you can facilitate your transactions and save more of your most valuable asset: time.

In the next chapter, I take you deeper into this concept and give you strategies for working with and negotiating with buyers.

CHAPTER **2 5**

Working and Negotiating with Buyers

*He who has learned to disagree without being disagreeable has discovered
the most valuable secret of a diplomat.*

—ROBERT ESTABROOK

Not everyone will jump on every deal you try to sell. But there is power in presenting
an opportunity and then quickly taking it away again. When you use this strategy, you
create the fear of loss among your potential buyers, and that puts you in a position to
sell more deals quickly. It puts you in a powerful negotiating position.

You've already learned how to negotiate with sellers. Negotiating with buyers
follows a lot of the same rules. Your ability to successfully negotiate and, more importantly, to understand the key time points at which to negotiate during a transaction
will determine your profitability on any given deal.

In this chapter, we'll focus on developing your ability to read and understand
other investors, and how you can use that knowledge to build rapport, create mutual
respect, and negotiate your way to a win-win transaction with the investors buying your
wholesale deals.

KNOW THE COMPARABLE SALES IN THE AREA

When wholesaling a property it's imperative to have a strong understanding of what
similar properties have sold in the area over the last six months. This will be something
buyers will often question you on when they are negotiating. Often, they will attempt
to use inadequate comparables to help negotiate a lower purchase price. It's your job to
know the surrounding market front and back so you can address these concerns right
out of the gate with confidence and reassurance that your valuation is correct.

Prior to presenting a wholesale deal to potential buyers you need to make sure
you've done your homework. The best evaluation method is to look at an area with a

three-tiered approach. You want to focus on what has happened in the past six months, what is happening today, and what will happen in the future to area values within a 0.5–1 mile radius.

Most wholesalers only focus on properties that have sold in the last six months. Although that is very important to know, it is equally important to have an understanding of what is currently under contract and what is actively listed for sale. Reviewing active listings and properties under contract will give you a glimpse into the next three-to-six months.

Part of being a great wholesaler is being able to explain the trends in an area. If you know what the closed sales are for the past six months, and roughly what the upcoming sales will be in the next six months, you will be able to paint the picture and justify your valuation if need be.

Knowing if values are on the rise in an area could be the single most important negotiation tool you have when dealing with an inexperienced buyer. Making a buyer feel comfortable with your experience may be the difference between your selling a wholesale property or not.

HAVE AN ACCURATE REPAIR COST

Proper due diligence and understanding the property you're selling allows you to articulate what is wrong with the house and what needs to be improved prior to resale. It is important for you to know how much it will cost to make those improvements, how long those improvements will take, and more importantly, what the property will sell for once these steps are taken. Knowing what is wrong with the house you are selling and having the ability to provide a brief description is a huge part of enticing your buyer to purchase the property.

I typically make a detailed repair list of exactly what needs to be done to the property. I then send that repair list to potential buyers as part of my Wholesale Deal Marketing Package. You might also consider having a trusted contractor give you a quote on that work. Having a contractor that is ready, willing, and able to start renovating the home is a major selling point, especially for inexperienced buyers. The more you can make the wholesale deal a turnkey situation, the more likely you are to sell it.

As a general rule of thumb, shy away from round numbers such as $20,000 in repairs or $30,000 in work needed. This immediately indicates to the buyer that little thought was put into the quote and it is probably inaccurate. You want the buyer to see a figure that is well thought through and crunched down to the penny, such as $27,450.

Utilizing this strategy will minimize many of the objections you may otherwise receive on the accuracy of the cost to repair the property.

When determining construction costs for a home it's important your improvements are in alignment with others in the neighborhood. For example, if you're quoting granite counters and the others in the area are selling with laminate counters, then you could be over-improving the property. Knowing what is the "norm" for an area will give you leverage in your negotiations when the buyer's quote accounts for items that would not be typical to the neighborhood. Remember, making yourself the expert on the product will give you the upper hand when negotiating.

CREATE A SENSE OF URGENCY

Probably the single most important component when selling a wholesale property is to create urgency when speaking to or meeting with the buyer. Creating fear of loss in a buyer is a very powerful tool, and if you use it correctly, it can help you seal the deal.

All successful people know how to make decisions promptly. The problem is that when most people are presented with an opportunity, they hesitate, and when you hesitate too long you often miss out on something incredible. We all know people who cannot make their own decisions—the ones who want to check with their wife, brother, uncle, or cousin's dog.

These people typically do not take action and no money is ever made by simply talking about it. More importantly, people like this will take as much time and money away from you as you let them. This is why you need to create a sense of urgency with each and every deal you handle. Opportunities to make money do not last long and this point should be made clear to every one of your potential buyers. All human decisions are helped with momentum; use urgency to help push the buyer into making a decision one way or another.

COMMON NEGOTIATING TECHNIQUES BUYERS USE

When negotiating it's important to know what questions you're going to get prior to receiving them. The more comfortable you are with your response, the better your chances are of coming out on top. What you'll find is there aren't too many tactics you will need if you have presented the buyer with all the information she needs to make a decision.

The most common technique is the straightforward approach. The buyer will come right out and ask you what is your bottom line on the property, or how much wiggle room is there. When you're faced with questions you need to hold firm to your set price and stress urgency because of the amount of activity you're getting on the home already.

An example of a follow-up response would be, "I understand you want to get the best deal you can, and I respect that, and I'm sure you can see I priced it very fairly and left plenty of profit in there for an investor like yourself. That said, the price is very firm." Saying the price is very firm still leaves you room to negotiate later on if need be.

The next tactic you may encounter is when the buyer attempts to use the "I-can't-make-the-numbers-work" scenario. This is typically when the buyer will test your knowledge base and throw out a low sales price of a property in the area in an attempt to lower your projected after-repair value and ultimately their purchase price. If you're adequately prepared, this is easy to overcome; if you're not, it can severely impact your sales price. A top negotiator will know this is coming and be able to respond to that one property as an anomaly and be able to redirect the focus.

Often, it's a property that may be smaller, in greater disrepair, on a bad street, or on an unappealing lot. Whatever the case may be, this should have popped up in your initial search for comparable properties and you have to have a meaningful response to the concern.

WHAT IF THE BUYER THINKS YOU'RE MAKING TOO MUCH?

If the buyer brings up the question of what you bought the property for and thinks you're making too much money on the transaction, then the focus should be redirected on them. If I'm directly questioned about my profit margin, I may play dumb and kindly ask, "Oh, is the profit margin not enough for you to consider purchasing?" Statements like this will place the focus back on the buyer and off of you and your profits.

Often, questions like these come about because you haven't taken the time to build adequate phone rapport or justified your value. Letting the buyers know you are in this to develop a long-term relationship where you can provide them with a lot of properties in the future, and possibly even be a buyer for them, is a great way to avoid these frustrating questions.

CONFIRM FUNDING

Your initial conversation should uncover which type of funding, whether cash, private money loan, hard-money loan, or traditional bank financing, is being used. It's best to reconfirm at the property; if the buyer is showing any interest in the home, always ask again what his or her lending source is going to be. Regardless of the type of funding, it's imperative you get some sort of *proof-of-funds letter* from the buyer's bank or funding source prior to signing any contract. The last thing you want is to tie up your wholesale with someone who may not be able to secure funding.

When a buyer is using a traditional lender you will have to do a lot more due diligence on your end. The first thing you need to do is pick up the phone and call the lender and make sure this client is approved to purchase for the amount the person is offering. You will often find out how well qualified this client is within the first minute or two of the conversation. You don't want a buyer who is teetering on the line of being approved or not being approved.

After learning more information about the buyer, let's assume you are working with a very qualified individual who seemingly will not have an issue getting approved for a loan. That said, it's just as important to interview the lender and make sure you have a clear understanding of what the bank's underwriting policies are. Some banks will not underwrite a loan if the contract has been sold to the buyer, so definitely be aware of that.

CASE STUDY

Not too long ago, I was speaking with one of our students, Anthony Moore, who is a very knowledgeable investor from Charlotte, North Carolina. He was telling me about a recent wholesale deal and how his knowledge of the market was really the key to putting the entire deal together with the buyer.

Anthony's buyer was a relatively new investor in the area and attempted several times to buy the property at a much lower price, stating the after-repair value was lower than what Anthony was quoting. Luckily, knowing the lack of similar comparables would be an issue, Anthony was able to show market trends in the area that would suggest values were rising considerably each month, and by the time they relisted the home the resale value he projected would be spot on. Because of his superior market knowledge Anthony was able to sell his contract for a $10,000 profit.

The buyer renovated the property and three months later sold the property for a $30,000 profit. This was one of the buyer's very first deals and a true win-win situation. The seller was so pleased, not only did she write Anthony a testimonial letter thanking his firm for its professionalism, but she also came back to view the home after it was renovated by the new buyers.

CONCLUSION

Successful negotiation hinges on thorough preparation. If you know the values of comparable sales in the area, and if you can give your investors an accurate estimate of what the repair cost should be, you will have more confidence when you are negotiating with buyers. The more knowledge you have, the more you'll have the upper hand in any negotiation.

Finally, never forget that you have what the buyer wants: a real estate deal that can be bought at a good price. In the next chapter I'll walk you through the first way you profit by wholesaling real estate—selling a contract.

CHAPTER **2 6**

How You Profit

Selling a Contract

You don't close a sale; you open a relationship if you want to build a long-term successful enterprise.

—Patricia Fripp

Successful investors always begin with the end in mind. We don't go into a negotiation without having an *exit strategy* waiting in the wings. We know that doing that is the equivalent of playing poker without being able to see some of your cards. From the very beginning, we think about how we are going to profit on the deal.

As a wholesaler, the two most common ways to close a deal are *selling a contract* and *double closing*. We'll talk about double closing in the next chapter.

Your first option is sell your contract to another buyer. Sometimes people refer to selling your contract as an *assignment*, or *assignment of contract*. This chapter will take you through the process of selling your wholesale deal straight to another investor.

WHAT DOES IT MEAN TO "SELL A CONTRACT"?

When you sell a contract you are not selling the property itself—you are actually selling your contract to another buyer. Under what is known as the *doctrine of equitable conversion*, once a real estate purchase agreement is signed by all parties and becomes effective, the buyer becomes the equitable owner and the seller retains bare legal title to the property under the terms of the agreement.

Said more simply, once you sign a contract to purchase a property, you have what is typically referred to as an *equitable interest* in the property. You don't have title to the property; you control it by means of a contract. When you sell your contract you are actually selling your rights within the terms of the contract to another buyer.

As mentioned earlier, when you sell a contract you aren't selling the property itself, you're merely selling your *contractual interest* in the property. You will never take title to the property, nor will you show up in the chain of title. You also won't be funding the deal. Your new buyer will pay you a profit for stepping into your shoes and will be the one who actually funds and closes the deal.

As discussed in the chapter about purchase and sale agreements, all purchase and sale agreements, by default, can be sold to another party unless specifically stated otherwise within the agreement. This is why it is very important to read the purchase and sale agreement you will be signing with the seller. Ideally, you want an experienced real estate attorney to review the agreement you plan on using for your deals to make sure it is worded correctly.

That being said, there are some state Board of Real Estate Agents contracts that specifically have a clause that limits your ability to sell or assign the contract; make sure you familiarize yourself with the agreements real estate agents are typically using in your area. If you do find a contract with a clause that prohibits you from assigning the contract, then you will have to modify the agreement or use a different purchase and sale agreement.

You can strike the clause directly from the agreement if both parties agree to it. This does not mean selling a contract is illegal—it is simply limited within the particular agreement you may be using. Once you have a legal and binding purchase and sale agreement, you can begin the process of looking for a buyer.

COMPLETING THE ASSIGNMENT OF REAL ESTATE PURCHASE AND SALE AGREEMENT

Once you have located a buyer and have agreed upon a price he is going to pay you for the contract, you will then execute an *Assignment of Real Estate Purchase and Sale Agreement*.

Remember, you are assigning your contractual rights to the new buyer for a profit. The new buyer is assuming all of your duties and obligations that you agreed upon in the purchase and sale agreement with the seller. This means the buyer must purchase the property at the agreed-upon price and closing date stipulated in the purchase and sale agreement.

In a typical Assignment of Real Estate Purchase and Sale Agreement, the investor who is selling the contract is considered to be the *assignor* and the new buyer is the *assignee*.

Obviously, there are many different Assignment of Real Estate Purchase and Sale Agreements that you can use. It is best to have an attorney review the agreement you plan on using to make sure that it is written correctly for what you are trying to accomplish.

It is very important is that you attach a copy of the purchase and sale agreement to the Assignment of Real Estate Purchase and Sale Agreement as Exhibit A. You never want the new buyer to say he didn't get a copy or didn't understand the terms of the original purchase and sale agreement. You should also attach any and all disclosures or other addendums that were made part of the purchase and sale agreement.

HOW DO YOU GET PAID?

This is the million-dollar question that every new wholesaler who is selling a contract wants to know. The terms of how you will get paid will also be spelled out in the Assignment of Real Estate Purchase and Sale Agreement and can happen in a number of ways. Everything is negotiable and up to you and the new buyer.

Typically, you will get a deposit when you sign the Assignment of Real Estate Purchase and Sale Agreement. Then when the transaction closes you will receive the rest of your profit. This is usually what the new buyer will want because he wants to make sure that the transaction closes before you get all of your money.

COORDINATING THE CLOSING

Just because you are not the one taking title and funding the transaction doesn't mean you don't have additional work to complete to make sure the deal gets closed. Once you find a buyer to whom you are going to sell your contract you have to make sure he follows through. You want to make sure the buyer understands the terms of the original purchase and sale agreement and closes on time.

This is why it is important to have a good title company and/or attorney handling the closing. Ideally, you also have a strong relationship with whoever is handling the closing so you can stay in touch and make sure the closing doesn't get delayed. You never know what is going to happen when the new buyer pulls title, especially when you are dealing with motivated sellers in financial distress.

If you live in a state where it's common practice to use a title company for the escrow and closing, then you want to make sure your title agent also understands these types of wholesale transactions. I also recommend that you have a very knowledgeable and experienced real estate attorney on your team in case you ever need help explaining the terms of the transaction to another Realtor, buyer, or lender. In some states your attorney can also be the one to handle the closing itself, depending on where you are doing business.

COMMON QUESTIONS

New investors always ask me whether the seller is going to have an issue with the contract being sold to another party. Of course, this will totally depend on the personality of the seller and your communication with him. This is rarely an issue if you communicate well with the seller.

The seller has signed a legal and binding purchase and sale agreement and is obligated to sell the property under the terms of the contract. You also have every legal right to sell or assign the contract to another party for a profit. The buyer you sell the contract to also has legal recourse and could sue the seller for specific performance if the seller walked away from the closing table and refused to sell the contract.

The majority of sellers you deal with will not have an issue with another buyer or entity closing on the property. Sellers usually only care about two things: that they walk away from the closing with a check for exactly what they thought they were going to get, and that the transaction closes on the agreed-upon date.

WHICH IS THE BETTER EXIT STRATEGY: SELLING A CONTRACT OR DOUBLE CLOSING?

This decision will depend on many factors. First, it will depend on the size of the profit. If you have a great deal and you find a buyer who is willing to pay you a lot more for the property, I would recommend that you double close on the property. When you're selling a contract there is always the small chance the seller could chose to walk away because she doesn't like seeing you make a profit on her property. When you sell a contract your profit will be disclosed to the seller as a line item on the HUD-1 or settlement statement. The negative is that you will incur additional closing expenses when you double close on a property.

Second, it will depend on how your buyer plans on financing the deal. If your buyer has a bank lending him money and you are selling your contract, you have to make sure you check with the buyer's lender to make sure there is nothing prohibiting you from doing so. Some banks have underwriting guidelines where they won't loan money if the contract is getting assigned. Other banks don't have an issue with it.

Finally, you must consider how long it will take your buyer to get his funding together. If he can't do it before the closing date stipulated on the purchase and sale agreement, then chances are you will have to close on the property and then resell it once the new buyer gets her funding lined up.

Once again, the majority of investors we prefer to sell contracts to are cash buyers and will fund the deal without having to deal with a bank. This makes wholesale transactions so much easier.

COMMON MISCONCEPTIONS ABOUT WHOLESALING

There are a lot of common misconceptions about selling contracts and wholesaling in general. Chances are you will run across a real estate agent who thinks it is illegal or that you are an unlicensed individual acting as an agent. The reality is there are a lot of agents, brokers, and attorneys who have never heard of wholesaling and who have very little real estate contract law experience. There is nothing illegal about selling a contract and you are not acting as an unlicensed agent.

You are the *buyer who is principal* to the transaction and you are *selling your contract* to another buyer. You are *not listing the property for a commission* like an agent. If you encounter someone who thinks what you are doing is illegal, you have to educate the person on what you do, how these transactions work, and your knowledge of real estate contracts. This is also why you want to be completely transparent about your role in the transaction whenever you're dealing with agents, brokers, and attorneys. This is also why it is good to have a knowledgeable real estate attorney who can explain the transaction to anyone you are working with.

CONCLUSION

Selling your contracts is a very powerful wealth-building strategy that doesn't require a lot of capital to get started. But it isn't the only way you stand to profit from wholesaling your deals.

In the next chapter, we look at the second way to close a wholesale transaction: double closing.

Coaching Student Success Story

FIGURE 26.1 Coaching Student Jenna Rouse
Reproduced by permission of Jenna Rouse.

Coaching Student Name: Jenna Rouse
Property Location: Connellsville, PA
Purchase Price: $8,000
Sale Price: $17,000
Profit: $9,000

Student Story: Just over nine months ago Jenna Rouse joined our coaching program. At the time, she was brand new to real estate investing. Since then she has wholesaled and rehabbed over 10 properties and is currently rehabbing multiple projects. She has long surpassed the income of her prior jobs and is now providing a better lifestyle for her daughter.

    Deal Summary: Jenna got the lead on this property from a bandit sign campaign she executed. The property had been in the seller's family for decades and more than 100 years earlier had served as a former train station, which was followed by a country store, a restaurant, and a single family residence. There was an addition built onto the main structure of the house that had fire damage—and the seller just wanted to wash his hands of the property. Jenna got the property under contract for $8,000.

FIGURE 26.2   Real Estate Deal in Connellsville, PA
Reproduced by permission of Jenna Rouse.

She then marketed the property online and to her buyers' list and got quite a few interested parties to contact her. She ended up "selling the contract" to another one of our coaching students for a $9,000 profit. The deal was very smooth because of the education and coaching she received on how to sell contracts.

For more information about our coaching go to: www.FortuneBuildersMastery .com.

Any income or earnings statements are estimates of income potential only and there is no assurance that your earnings will match the figures presented. Any income or earnings depicted are not to be interpreted as common, typical, expected, or normal for the average person.

How You Profit

Double Closing

If we learn from losing, we become winners in the end.

—Anonymous

Selling a contract to make a profit can be a great option for you as a wholesaler. But it's not always the best option available to you. In some scenarios, another solution is on the table that gives you even more of an edge. That solution is double closing on the property.

Double closings are very common in the real estate investing world. However, not all agents, brokers, attorneys, or title companies have dealt with them or understand how they work. As a wholesaler, having a strong grasp of the nature of this transaction puts you in a position to explain it to any other party involved in the deal. The more you know, the more deals you will sell at the end of the day.

WHAT IS A DOUBLE CLOSING?

A *double closing*, or *back-to-back closing*, is when you purchase a property and then resell it fairly quickly without rehabbing the property. This could be hours, days, or weeks later. It is not very different from the way you would normally buy and sell a property; it just happens on a much quicker timeline.

When you double close there are two transactions that take place. The first transaction is between you and the seller, often called the *A-B* transaction. The second transaction is between you and the new buyer, or the *B-C* transaction. You will open two escrows and have two separate settlement statements.

The *settlement statement* is a document summarizing all the fees and charges that both the buyer and seller face during the settlement process of a real estate transaction.

This form, which is under the jurisdiction of the U.S. Department of Housing and Urban Development, is also known as the *HUD-1*.

The first settlement statement will be between you and the seller, the A-B transaction, where the numbers reflect the original sale price that was negotiated. The second settlement statement reflects the new sale price between you and your new buyer, the B-C transaction.

The biggest difference between selling a contract and double closing is that in the latter you are actually selling the *property* instead of the contract. You will, for a very short period of time, be the owner of the property, and you will show up in the chain of title. You will also incur closing expenses, both when you buy and when you sell, which will take away from the overall profitability of the deal.

However, the amount of fees incurred will vary depending on the type of property you are purchasing, the price you're paying for the property, the state you are closing in, the title company you are using, and what you negotiate.

The key to performing a successful double closing is to understand whom you are buying from and the terms of the original purchase and sale agreement. Second, you must know how your buyer plans on funding the deal and what type of lender she is using (if any) so you can make sure the second purchase and sale agreement is structured correctly and will actually close.

Finally, you must understand the timeline and be able to coordinate all of the different parties involved. It's not rocket science, but it's definitely not as easy as the standard transaction most real estate professionals and title companies are used to.

SIGNING THE FIRST PURCHASE AND SALE AGREEMENT ON THE A-B TRANSACTION

The first thing you need to be aware of is whom you are buying the property from and what type of purchase and sale agreement they want to use if it's not yours. If you are dealing with a seller and it's not a short sale or a bank REO, it's pretty straightforward.

If it is a short sale, you have to check the terms within the bank's *short-sale acceptance letter* to see if they have any type of short-term resale or deed restriction. Some lenders will place a 30-, 60-, or 90-day resale restriction into the terms. Not all lenders have these, but you definitely have to read everything within the short-sale acceptance letter to see if they do. If the lender does have a deed restriction, it will say something like:

> The purchaser cannot resell the property within 30 days of the short sale settlement date. The purchaser cannot resell the property for greater than 120 percent of the short sale price within 90 days of the short sale settlement date.

This means two things. First, you can't sell the property until a minimum of 30 days after you close. Second, if you sell the property within 90 days, you can't sell it for more than 20 percent above what you paid for it.

What options do you have if you are looking to wholesale? First, you can attempt to negotiate the deed restriction; some banks will take it off their short-sale acceptance letter, but not many. Your other option is to hold the property and sell it once the deed restriction has expired. This will definitely eat into your profit so make sure the numbers still work if this is the case.

You might also consider doing a joint venture with the rehabber-investor who is buying the property from you and just take a portion of the profit applicable to what you were going to get paid if you want to start the work right away.

If you are buying a bank REO, you will not deal with as many deed restrictions. However, a lot of banks will have a clause in their contracts that stipulates that you can't assign the contract. In that case you will have to double close on the property with your new buyer.

SIGNING THE SECOND PURCHASE AND SALE AGREEMENT ON THE B-C TRANSACTION

In the previous chapter, we discussed how to sell a contract by filling out an Assignment of Real Estate Purchase and Sale Agreement. When you double close you will not be utilizing this form. You will actually be entering into a *second* purchase and sale agreement with your new buyer that is *contingent* on the first closing (A-B) actually taking place.

Thus, you must clearly disclose within the agreement that there is another agreement that must close before this agreement can move forward. Likewise, you must fully and fairly disclose to all parties in the second transaction about the first escrow. The last thing you want is to have the deal blow up because the agent, buyer, or the buyer's lender wasn't aware of the first transaction. You also don't want anyone questioning your actions because you didn't disclose the nature of the transaction. Always practice full disclosure.

If you have never performed a double closing, you should absolutely consult with a real estate attorney and make sure they double-check your paperwork before you sign the second purchase and sale agreement. If you're in a state where you close with a title company, you should call the title agent and go through the nature of the transaction in order to make sure the agent understands it.

There are a few title companies that will shy away from these transactions because they only like easy, traditional transactions and anything out of the ordinary scares them. This does not mean double closings are illegal or that you can't find a title company to close the transaction. It's just something to be aware of.

KNOW HOW THE BUYER IN THE B-C TRANSACTION IS PLANNING ON FUNDING THE DEAL BEFORE YOU SIGN A SECOND PURCHASE AND SALE AGREEMENT

Years ago, we ended up having a wholesale deal blow up because I didn't check the buyer's funding source. The buyer had told me he was going to use his cash to fund the deal, but I never asked him for a proof of funds. Well, two days before the closing I called the buyer and found out that he didn't actually have the money and that his "private lender" had fallen through.

At the time, we didn't have another plan so we ended up closing on the property not knowing whether this buyer would come through. Well, the buyer backed out of the agreement and we were forced to rehab a property we didn't think we were going to have to rehab.

In the end, it worked out fine because we made a decent profit. However, the opportunity cost was huge because we literally spent weeks trying to get this buyer funded. So learn from my mistakes and *always* double-check the buyer's funding source.

Ideally, you want to sell the majority of your wholesale deals to cash buyers whose funding you have verified because you won't have to deal with a lender on the second transaction. Cash buyers and buyers with private lenders are so much easier to deal with and the transactions are so much smoother for the title company or closing attorney.

If your C buyer is using a hard-money lender, you definitely want to call the lender and explain the transaction so the lender is aware it will be a double closing situation.

Most hard-money lenders are very aware of wholesaling and the nature of the transactions, so there isn't much to worry about.

If your C buyer is planning on getting funding from a traditional lender, you have to call and make the lender aware that this is a double escrow situation. Some lenders have *title seasoning* requirements and will only fund borrowers who are buying a property from someone who has been on title for a certain number of months. Most property seasoning requirements by Fannie Mae and Freddie Mac have been removed, other than for certain cash-out refinance programs.

The Federal Housing Administration (FHA), on the other hand, has property seasoning waivers for transactions that meet requirements, which means the borrower and/or seller will need to document their case for the increase in value on the unseasoned property.

An *unseasoned property*, or one that goes from one person to another in a short period of time, will generally get a much closer examination by the underwriter to ensure that the loan is not a fraud. Many wholesale lenders have stricter requirements for funding unseasoned properties. Typically, these are called *overlays* because they are stricter underwriting guidelines placed over their normal guidelines. The reason lenders do this is because most loans are sold on the secondary market, and if a borrower defaults on the mortgage during a certain time period, the lender will actually have to repurchase the mortgage.

The bottom line is *call the lender* and make sure you talk to the underwriter together before you ever sign a second purchase and sale agreement with your C buyer if the buyer is getting traditional bank financing.

If the lender won't fund the transaction, then you will have to convince the buyer to use cash or a private lender, or get them in touch with a good local hard-money lender.

WHAT ELSE TO LOOK FOR FROM YOUR C BUYER

When you are dealing with an investor as opposed to a retail buyer, you need to be much stricter on the terms of the contract and the deposit. When you're going to sign a second purchase and sale agreement with your C buyer make sure the deposit is sizeable enough so that the investor has something on the line and doesn't walk away.

Likewise, you will compare the strength and terms of the different offers you get from investors. You should be very clear in your communication to investors that you expect very few contingencies within the contract. I recommend that *inspection contingencies* be no longer than 72 hours when you are dealing with an investor. You should expect the investors you deal with to be knowledgeable enough and comfortable enough with their deposit "going hard" after a very short period of time. This means the deposit would be nonrefundable if your C buyer didn't close. The last thing you want to deal with is an investor backing out of the deal weeks after you have signed a contract with him.

On properties you are wholesaling, the only time you would sign a contract with financing contingencies is if you have a flexible seller and you have spoken with the lender who is representing the buyer and you have verified all the terms. Even with a substantial deposit, you always want to make sure that you verify everything with the lender and that he understands the nature of the transaction.

DON'T PASS FUNDING THROUGH

It is important to note that you can't *pass through* or use your C buyer's funding to close the initial purchase if the buyer purchasing the property from you is getting a bank loan. This means you will have to fund the initial A-B purchase when you close on the property. If you don't have cash readily available, the best strategy is to utilize a private lender, transactional lender, or hard-money lender who will provide you the short-term funding you need to close the A-B transaction.

The lenders will generally only have their money in the deal for a very short period of time until you sell the property to your new buyer. Typically, you will find private lenders who will charge you one or two points for short-term funding. There are also transactional lenders and hard-money lenders who fund these short-term transactions at two or three points. Of course, if you can't find a good lender, you could always go visit Vinnie, your local mob boss and loan shark. The going rate for Vinnie's money is usually 10 to 20 points. He probably won't even ask you for a personal guarantee.

ALWAYS HAVE LEGAL COUNSEL

Always remember to make sure to obtain advice from a real estate attorney who understands creative real estate transactions. Some attorneys may not be well versed in structuring creative real estate deals and may not know how to give the proper guidance on certain transactions. Do some research to find a very experienced real estate attorney who can assist you throughout the process.

CONCLUSION

When you understand the various purchase scenarios you can enter into, as well as the various types of buyers you will be dealing with when you enter into them, you empower yourself to choose the best way to close a deal. In the next chapter, I'll walk you through the closing process itself to bring you full circle on taking a wholesaling deal from start to finish.

Coaching Student Success Story

FIGURE 27.1   Coaching Student Dan Robles
Reproduced by permission of Daniel Robles.

Coaching Student's Name: Dan Robles
Property Location: Bloomington, California
Purchase Price: $37,727
Holding Costs: $1,734
Sale Price: $95,000
Gross Profit: $55,538

(continued)

(continued)

Student Story: Dan Robles had a background in finance when he joined our coaching program. He currently has multiple real estate projects going on and just recently transitioned out of his day-to-day job to focus on his real estate investment company full time.

Deal Summary: This property was scheduled for a tax sale when Dan tracked down the owners' mailing address since they did not live at the property. Dan actually tried to find the owners, but the day he went they weren't home, so he left some information about his company and how he could help them avoid the tax sale.

FIGURE 27.2   Real Estate Deal in Bloomington, CA
Reproduced by permission of Daniel Robles.

About a month-and-a-half later the owners finally contacted Dan via phone and asked him for more information about the tax sale they were unaware of. Dan offered them $38,000 for the property, which completely paid off the tax lien and gave them an additional $8,000 on top of that.

The owners of the property were very thankful because they did not want the property to go to sale. Dan had to close relatively quickly because the pending sale was not too far off. He originally planned on rehabbing the property. However, soon thereafter, Dan was approached by a local investor-contractor who had been trying to purchase the property for over two years. The investor expressed a high level of interest and offered Dan $95,000 for the property. Dan ended up double closing on the property and made $56,000 on the deal.

For more information about our coaching go to: www.FortuneBuildersMastery .com.

Any income or earnings statements are estimates of income potential only and there is no assurance that your earnings will match the figures presented. Any income or earnings depicted are not to be interpreted as common, typical, expected, or normal for the average person.

The Real Estate Closing Process

The secret of a man's success resides in his insight into the moods of people, and his tact in dealing with them.

—J. G. HOLLAND

You've just run 25.5 miles of a 26-mile-long wholesaling marathon. When you reach the closing process, the finish line is in sight.

It starts when you sign an *assignment of contract* (or a second purchase and sale agreement) with your buyer. That signature is the first step of a complex process that ends with the close of the entire transaction—and a check for the deal in your hands.

The *closing process* officially starts when you open escrow with an escrow company, title company, or an attorney. In *escrow*, ownership of the property is transferred via the assistance of an impartial third party. Escrow is designed to minimize risk for both the buyer and the seller because the responsibility for handling the documents and funding is placed in the hands of someone not affected by the outcome of the transaction. Having an escrow minimizes the possibility of fraud or a violation of any terms of the agreement.

You will have to manage the closing process to make sure that your deal closes on time. For that reason, you need to be in constant communication with all parties involved in the transaction. And you need to understand how the closing process itself works.

WHO HANDLES THE ESCROW AND CLOSING?

This will depend on what state you are doing business in. In some states it's customary to have an escrow company or agency handle the closing. In other states title companies will have escrow offices within the company and under the same brand name. In some states, especially in the eastern part of the United States, attorneys will handle escrow and the closing. Finally, in a few states you can actually choose who handles escrow and use an attorney or an escrow company.

WHAT IS REQUIRED TO OPEN ESCROW?

To open escrow there are five basic requirements you must meet. You must have two competent parties, a valid contract, a property, mutual agreement as to the terms and conditions of the deal, and valid consideration in the form of money, promissory note, or anything of value offered by one party and accepted by the other.

Typically, once you have a written purchase and sale agreement you or your real estate agent will open escrow. There are some states where it is typical to open escrow later in the process; however, in most areas you open it right away. Usually, you will start the escrow process by sending over the purchase and sale agreement, the assignment of contract if there is one, and written escrow and closing instructions. Generally, you will have one set of *escrow instructions* between the seller and the escrow company. You will then have another set of escrow instructions between the buyer and the escrow company. Finally, if the buyer is using a lender, there will be another set of instructions between the borrower and lender. In some states they have joint escrow instructions, which would be for the buyer and seller together.

When the escrow instructions are properly written and signed by both parties and returned to the escrow company, then the escrow is officially open. The escrow instructions also become binding contracts that are fully enforceable in a court of law. This means you, the seller, and the buyer must comply with the terms of the contracts you have signed and the closing agent must comply with the terms written in the closing instructions.

Keeping track of all aspects of a deal can be a difficult task and good organizational skills can begin with a simple checklist. When you open escrow you will also want to provide escrow with a take sheet. A *take sheet* is essentially a checklist of items the closing agent will need to know. This includes information about the property, the seller, buyer, real estate agents and commissions, existing loans, new loans, title company information, and proration information. To download an example take sheet that you can modify, go to www.TheWholesalingBible.com.

Once you have opened escrow, your escrow will be assigned a file number and then assigned to an escrow or closing officer. Depending on what state you do business in, this person could be called an *escrow officer, escrow agent, closing agent, title officer, settlement agent*, or *attorney*. In this chapter I refer to this individual as a *closing agent* to avoid confusion.

WHO SELECTS THE ESCROW COMPANY?

Local customs and real estate practices usually dictate how the escrow company or holder is selected. For example, in California, it depends on what part of the state you live in. In Southern California, the seller usually selects the escrow company. In Northern California, it is typical for the buyer to select the escrow company. If an agent is involved in the transaction, the agent usually will be the one who suggests the escrow company. Remember, this is always negotiable, so ultimately it is up to you and whomever you are working with on the deal.

ARE YOU OPENING ONE ESCROW OR TWO?

As a wholesaler this will depend on whether you are selling the contract or doing a back-to-back closing. If you are selling the contract, you will only open one escrow. If you are planning on doing a back-to-back closing, you will actually open two escrows and the second one will be dependent on the first escrow. If you are using an escrow/title company to close the transaction, you must check with them to see if they are open to handling both escrows at the same time. Be aware that some escrow/title companies will want you to use a different escrow/title company for the second closing.

WHAT HAPPENS DURING ESCROW?

The closing agent has many duties once escrow is officially opened and before your deal actually closes. Here is short summary of what these agents handle:

- They gather escrow instructions and any missing information from all parties involved in the transaction.
- They issue receipts for any and all deposits of funds.
- They order a title search that is later compiled into a title report.
- They get payoff amounts together from all lenders who are owed money on the property. They also request releases from the lender for any mortgages or deeds of trust that must be paid off in escrow.

- They obtain any necessary documents to clear any other outstanding liens against the property.
- They obtain title insurance for the buyer and or the lender.
- They make sure the buyer obtains a new insurance policy.
- They prepare the final closing statements and prorate all taxes, interest, and rents.
- They prepare all the appropriate documents for the closing, obtain the proper signatures, and disburse all funds to the appropriate parties.
- They return loan packages to the lender with all the appropriate signatures.
- They record all the necessary documents, such as grant deeds, mortgages, deeds of trust, powers of attorney, and reconveyances.

The closing agent obviously has numerous responsibilities in order to prepare the closing. More importantly, her job is to be an impartial party who preserves the confidentiality of all the parties involved in the closing and who makes sure everyone is acting according to the escrow instructions.

HOW DO YOU PREPARE FOR CLOSING?

The closing agent or attorney is obviously doing most of the heavy lifting during the closing process. However, it is your job to be in constant communication with all the parties involved in the transaction and to make sure they are getting everything to the closing agent on time. Some closing agents are more proactive than others, so you should work very closely with them to make sure all documents get into them on time.

The most important thing is making sure that your buyer meets all his deadlines. Remember, the seller signed the original purchase and sale agreement with you and is expecting you to follow through on all of your promises. If you sold the contract to another buyer, he may not have the same sense of urgency as you, so it is your job to follow up with the buyer consistently and make sure everything is in place for the closing.

You may even find yourself helping out in ways you didn't expect. For example, when we are working with buyers who don't have a lot of good relationships we often help them find good contractors to work with. If the buyer is really new, we have even helped him formulate a complete scope of work on the property. A *scope of work* is essentially an instruction set the contractors use to make their bids where you outline exactly what you expect to be done to the property and what type of materials you want to use.

There are multiple considerations and challenges associated with every closing. Personalities, details, legalities, formalities, and specific key components must be addressed during the course of any wholesale transaction.

WHAT CAN CAUSE DELAYS DURING THE CLOSING PROCESS?

There are a lot of things that can cause delays during the closing process. This is why it is so important to stay in touch with the closing agent throughout the escrow period in case something pops up that is unexpected. Here are a few common things that may occur during the closing.

- *Slow title work:* If you have to close in a very short time period, make sure the agent puts a rush on ordering the title search. There may be an extra expense for this, but you don't want the title search to slow down the closing. A title search may make you aware of liens or encumbrances that will need to be paid off or cleared before title can transfer.
- *Unexpected liens:* When you are working with property owners in financial distress you have to expect items to pop up on title that they may not have disclosed. We have often had to step in and negotiate with junior lien holders at the last minute because they popped up on title. You will also find that sometimes the seller owes more on the property than the price you have put it under contract for, so make sure you review the title work when it comes back.
- *Delayed payoffs:* Title problems and delays in getting payoffs are the two main reasons for postponements of closings. In order to minimize these delays and gain added control of the process, it is crucial to take a proactive role in resolving conflicts and clearing up issues. Many investors make the mistake of handing off the complete file to the closing agent and expecting the deal to close smoothly with no further intervention on their part.
- *Buyer funding issues:* If the buyer is not using cash to purchase the property, you have to monitor the closing much more closely. If the buyer is using a lender of any sort, make sure the lender understands the nature of the transaction and that it doesn't violate any of the lender's underwriting guidelines. Ideally, you want to speak to the buyer's lender before you sign the assignment of contract or a second purchase

and sale agreement. However, I have had lenders ask a lot more questions and have extra stipulations when it is a wholesale deal I am purchasing and then immediately reselling. Often, they require a second appraisal at the last minute, so be prepared for this if your buyer is not using cash.

- *Lack of communication between parties:* Coordinating a closing is similar to coaching a sports team or conducting a symphony orchestra. There are multiple members of your closing team who each have independent responsibilities. However, this doesn't mean they always communicate properly. You will often find that a real estate agent thought the closing agent was going to handle something and vice versa, and then a day or two before the closing, tensions rise when something needed for the closing is not available. It is your job to make sure these individuals come together as a team and remain in-sync in order to be successful. As the coach and conductor, your role is to make certain that everyone is doing their job and meeting their deadlines.

Pay very close attention to the seller. A lot of sellers are nervous about every step of the transaction; from the very start to the time they sign the sale contract and all the way through to closing. They are a ticking bomb composed of fear, distrust, anxiety, and distractions surrounding and worrying them into a near frenzy. In the majority of instances, sellers will question whether they've made the right decision right up until they sign on the dotted line on the day of closing. It is your job to manage the seller's expectations throughout the process. Maintain frequent contact with the seller and keep him or her current and up to date on timelines, delays, negotiations, and all other aspects of the deal.

WHAT TO CHECK THE DAY BEFORE CLOSING

The day before closing you want to ensure that everything is ready for the closing taking place the next day:

- Call the closing agent to confirm the time and location of the closing.
- Let the seller and buyer know the time and location of the closing.
- Request a preliminary or final closing statement if there is one.
- Confirm that the buyer's funding is in escrow unless the buyer is bringing funds to the closing.
- Review closing figures for any mistakes.
- Confirm insurance, deeds, trust deeds, and mortgage documents are correct.
- Do a final walkthrough of the property with the buyer, if necessary.

WHAT TAKES PLACE AT THE CLOSING?

The *closing* is when the actual exchange of money for the deed to the property takes place. The buyer will sign all the closing documents and release the money she is using to purchase the property. The seller will then sign a deed legally transferring ownership to the buyer. Depending on the closing agent's requirements for clearing funds, the actual release of funds to the seller may occur that day or a few days later. Once everything is signed, the deed will be recorded in the county recorder's office, along with any mortgage or deed-of-trust documents. The buyer will receive a title insurance policy that guarantees the title to the property is valid.

HOW TO ENSURE THERE ARE NO SNAGS THE DAY OF CLOSING

Managing the transaction on the day of the closing is as important as all the other steps leading to this point. It is vital to make the seller comfortable by creating the right environment for the closing. It is important for the person who has built the rapport with the seller to be present, so there is an instant familiarity and comfort level. Another very effective tactic to help maintain control of the closing is to keep the seller and the ultimate buyer separate.

HIRING SOMEONE TO HELP YOU PROCESS YOUR WHOLESALE DEALS

After you close a few wholesale deals you might consider hiring an assistant or someone who can help you process your transactions and manage the escrow process. For example, we have someone in our office whose only job is to process transactions, work with our escrow agent, and communicate with all the parties involved in the transaction. If you are thinking about hiring a processor, make sure this individual is extremely organized and ideally has some sort of escrow experience. You can easily find someone who is a former escrow agent or paralegal, or has worked at a title company, who could fill this role in your business.

CONCLUSION

Every party involved in the escrow has different responsibilities and it's your job to make sure everyone is meeting their deadlines. This is why it is extremely important to create closing checklists you can use to keep you organized and help save you and the closing agent time during the escrow process. There is a lot of information that needs to be gathered, explained, and given to the closing agent if you want the deal to close on time.

It's important to remember that every closing is unique. Never assume that everything is going to go according to plan. Stay on top of things, make sure that everyone is meeting their deadlines, and always expect the unexpected.

With closing, as with many other stages of the wholesaling process, having a dependable team in place will make the tasks and trials you face a lot easier to handle on a daily basis. In the next chapter, you will learn how to build a strong local team to help you grow your business.

CHAPTER 29

Building Your Local Team

The main ingredient of stardom is the rest of the team.

—John Wooden

I once worked with a buyer who was represented by a brand-new real estate agent. The deal I was wholesaling had a tremendous profit potential and the buyer I had lined up was extremely interested in it. But the deal required a double closing, and that was where we ran into trouble. The real estate agent had never heard of a double closing. I tried to explain the transaction to him, but he wasn't having any of it. "This sounds fishy," he told me. Then he went to the buyer and advised him not to sign my contract because, he said, he thought it might be illegal.

I didn't want to lose my buyer, but I'd done everything I could do to talk to this agent on my own. So I did the only thing left: I called my real estate attorney. If the neophyte agent wasn't going to listen to my explanation, maybe he would listen to someone who specialized in real estate law.

A day or two later, the rookie agent called me up. "I want to apologize," he said. "I'd never heard of a double closing before, but your attorney explained it to me. My client is ready to move forward with the deal." I didn't land that deal all on my own. I landed that deal because I had a knowledgeable teammate waiting in the wings.

If you plan to be successful in this business, you must have a support team of real estate professionals who are involved in your real estate deals. Your core team members include real estate agents, hard-money lenders, mortgage brokers, insurance agents, title agents, attorneys, and contractors.

The team members listed in this chapter don't work for you; they work *with* you. Although they have their own businesses, they are integral when it comes to closing your real estate transactions. Let's discuss the roles and responsibilities of these few key professionals, how they help your business, and exactly how to find the best of them so that you are free to sip piña coladas in the Bahamas while deals are being closed for you by your team.

REAL ESTATE AGENTS

A strong real estate agent is one of the most important members of any real estate investor's team, and a strong investor should be one of the most important members of an agent's team. Once you are able to establish a cohesive relationship, this powerful partnership will really start to blossom.

Many investors may wish to discard the notion of hiring an agent when they can get their license and just do the work themselves. While it is a smart idea to obtain your real estate license, working with additional agents can only help you and your business grow. As long as you keep an open mind, you can find competent, ethical, high-quality agents who will work very hard.

Some Advantages to Working with a Really Good Real Estate Agent

- *More time:* By adding quality agents to your team, you are freeing up time to get more deals because they can help you find buyers for your deals.
- *Deals:* Real estate agents can bring you high-quality deals and obviously have access to the Multiple Listing Service in your area if you don't.
- *Local market knowledge:* A really good agent will know a lot about the local market and can help you make key decisions about properties you are buying or selling.
- *Paperwork:* When you have an agent working with you, you avoid the time commitment of handling a lot of the necessary paperwork in the closing process.
- *Pocket listings:* Sometimes, by the time you see a "For Sale" sign on a property, it's already too late. Some agents will call their existing clients and let them know about deals that haven't even hit the market yet.
- *Selling properties:* Agents can market your property and take calls from prospective buyers and buyers' agents.

Think strategically when approaching your selection process. It's especially critical to establish relationships with a few of the top-producing real estate agents in your area. Top producers are the agents who get the majority of listings from banks and private sellers based on their relationships and years of experience. Top producers also have the biggest pool of potential buyers for your properties. Once you have a relationship with one of these agents, he or she will often let you know about a potential deal before it ever gets listed.

You will also want to work with at least three or four ambitious agents who may not yet be top producers, but who are willing to research potential investment properties for you. These agents will run sales comparables, view properties and make repair estimates, and drive the sales comparables to help you determine the after-repairs value so you can make an appropriate offer. These agents should be reliable, fast, and willing to learn your real estate investing process.

LOCATING THE TOP AGENTS IN YOUR MARKET

It's not very difficult to find a real estate agent. The key is to know who the top producers are in your area and to establish relationships with them. The easiest way to do this is to find out if the Multiple Listing Service tracks listing and sales volume in your area by agent identification number. Most MLS systems do track this by zip code, but you have to get the information through an agent who has access to the MLS. Some agents know how to do these searches and others don't.

Another option would be to call the Board of Realtors. The Board is not obligated to hand over the information; however, if you talk to the right person, you may end up getting it.

It's not essential, nor will it be possible, to establish a relationship with every single top producer. You are looking for a few long-term relationships that will lead to future deals. Agents should know who you are, and have an idea of your role in the market. This is essential if you want to create a dominant presence in an area.

Explain how you can be of benefit to an agent in the near future. We let all agents know exactly how we will become a valuable tool in their toolbox. We do this by explaining to them that many of our offers will be lower than other retail clients they might find; however, we come in as a great benefit for hard-to-sell properties or for those requiring the bank or seller to move quickly. We let agents know we are a good fit if they have properties that won't qualify for traditional financing based on their current condition. There are several benefits to working with investors, and all you're trying to do is establish that you are a serious buyer, that you are well financed, and that you could bring multiple commissions annually.

Some Benefits You Can Offer an Agent

- Gaining repeat business
- Opportunity to make both sides of the commission
- Becoming a distressed-property specialist
- Access to property inventory before it is listed
- Opportunity to host open houses
- Short-sale referrals

HARD-MONEY LENDERS

As discussed earlier, hard-money lenders are niche lenders who finance properties that most banks traditionally won't lend on. In exchange, hard-money lenders charge much higher interest rates and points, and have much shorter loan-length terms.

You should have one or two really good relationships with local hard-money lenders. You may need to first borrow from them on wholesale transactions that you have to fund before you end up selling to your end buyer. More importantly, though, you will have to refer a lot of your end buyers to a hard-money lender when you find buyers who don't have the cash to buy the property from you. When you establish a strong relationship with hard-money lenders, they may end up referring you quite a few buyers over the years. The relationship is worth its weight in gold.

MORTGAGE BROKERS

In addition to having a hard-money lender, you should have a good mortgage broker on your team to whom you can refer buyers in certain scenarios. The most important thing is that the mortgage broker understands the nature of back-to-back closings so he or she can find lenders who don't have title seasoning issues.

Your goal should be to work with one of the top mortgage brokers in the area—someone who is consistently closing loans with a wide variety of loan products. You can find top brokers through referrals from real estate agents, title companies, or other investors. Your mortgage broker has to have great telephone communication skills and the ability to promote relationships. It is not essential, but it is beneficial if the broker is local because he or she can also meet in person with clients you refer who need that personal touch.

INSURANCE AGENTS

One of the easier team members to find will be a good insurance agent. You can ask real estate agents, mortgage brokers, and other investors for referrals to insurance agents. The key is to choose an insurance agent who understands that you will be purchasing properties in need of significant work and holding them short term. The insurance policies you receive will be very different from the ones traditional homeowners receive because many of the properties you buy may not have working mechanicals; they may have structural issues and sometimes even cracked foundations.

TITLE AGENT/REAL ESTATE ATTORNEY

Depending on the states in which you are buying and selling, you will need a good title agent and/or closing attorney. Different states handle real estate closings in different ways. Find out the standard procedure in the state you'll be doing the most business in. Either way, it is important that you have an open line of communication with the person who is handling your closings, whether it's a title agent or a real estate attorney. This key team member must understand how to close transactions when you sell the contract and when you are doing a back-to-back closing, and should also understand creative financing techniques such as buying a property with owner financing or subject to the existing mortgage. Many of the properties sold have been owned for a very short period of time, so your title agent or attorney must understand the structure of your transactions.

Having a real estate attorney or title agent on your side can help to make sure your best interests are faithfully upheld and help navigate through difficulties you may encounter. A title agent protects homeowners and lenders against financial loss by thoroughly checking that a title is clear of all liens, judgments, or anything else that could affect it. They will protect your interest and assist you with problems with closing, should they occur.

The key is to find a title agent or attorney who performs regular closings with other experienced investors in your area. If you close in a state that traditionally utilizes attorneys to handle real estate closings, it is very important to make sure you work with an attorney who specializes in this form of law. Attorneys can have many different specialties. Just because a law firm handles real estate closings doesn't mean it specializes in them. Find a firm where at least half of the work is real estate related.

CONTRACTORS

All successful real estate wholesalers build relationships with contractors and contracting teams. When you're wholesaling a property, chances are you will be selling to another investor who will be rehabbing the property. Sometimes, when you're showing a property to a new rehabber, he won't have relationships with high-quality contractors; if you can make the introduction, it can facilitate an offer on your property.

CONCLUSION

Building rapport with your team of professionals is invaluable. It allows you to effectively communicate with people and to build interpersonal relationships. More, it enables you to work in a more cohesive and relaxed environment. Always ask experienced investors for recommendations when you start building your team, but never skip the step of interviewing an individual yourself before bringing him or her on board. Meeting potential team members in person is the best way to determine whether they'll work well with your personal business model.

Your local team is indispensable. But it's not the only team you need to have in place. The next chapter covers everything you need to know about building your business advisory team.

CHAPTER 30

Building Your Business Advisory Team

You don't need to know it all. You must assemble a team of experts that knows it all.

—J. D. ESAJIAN

As an athlete, I always appreciated having a coach who not only pushed me, but also strategically guided me as I set my goals and then worked toward achieving them. During my athletic career, I realized that my coaches could see what I wasn't able to see regarding my personal development, performance, and overall potential. With a few choice insights and practice sessions, they brought my contributions to the game to another level, a level I'd have been unable to reach on my own at that time.

When I was drafted by the Tampa Bay Buccaneers, my defensive backs coach was a man named Mike Thomlin. In the first two weeks of practice, with Mike's guidance, I learned more about the strategy of the game of football than I had in my previous 10 years of playing the sport. For example, he taught me how to anticipate the route one receiver was running based on the route the tight end or other receiver was running. By being able to see the bigger picture I was able to put myself in a better position to make a play.

By implementing what Mike taught me, I was able to raise the level of my performance so that I could compete with the other players, who often had superior athleticism. Mike has since gone on to become the Super Bowl–winning head coach of the Pittsburgh Steelers.

Through athletics, I also realized that coaches change the way you think. They have a plan for your development that ultimately could not be realized without them. In business, it is no different. The vast majority of Fortune 500 CEOs (men and women who lead the largest and most successful companies in the world) receive business and growth coaching. Many of these individuals are the highest earners on the planet, and many of them attribute their success to their openness toward learning.

Unfortunately, I've also encountered a few misguided people who believe they are admitting weakness if they seek coaching. Sadly, some individuals allow their egos or other people's perceptions of them to become a hindrance to their success. Can you imagine the owner of an NFL team deciding to go without coaches for a year just to save money? Obviously, that's absurd and would never happen. However, that is the exact choice some entrepreneurs and real estate investors make when they decide to start their businesses.

Coaching was important to me as an athlete because I always wanted to put myself in the best position to succeed in the shortest amount of time. And the same is true in the business world; it is beneficial to have a coach or someone who can advise you and hold you accountable to the goals you set for yourself.

When you work for yourself, it's up to you to determine what you want to accomplish every day. As an entrepreneur, you won't necessarily have someone looking over your shoulder and holding you accountable for your daily progress. That's why it's critical to establish a good support system.

Years ago, I decided to build a team of advisors to guide me as I grew my business. That was one of the best decisions I ever made. Over the years, this team has helped me make many strategic business decisions that I didn't necessarily have all the answers for. Having a team in place that could help me make these key decisions was a welcome relief to me. In a sense, this has been a form of intellectual leverage I have been able to tap into over the years.

There is so much to know about the real estate business and I knew that I didn't necessarily need to be the one to know it all. I had to assemble a team that I could rely on to get the answers I needed. I wasn't going to let my ego get in the way of my success.

The individuals on your advisory team will help you create an effective business model. They will push you to work more strategically and efficiently. They will answer your most pertinent real estate, business, tax, and legal questions. And they will help you make numerous key decisions along the way so that you work smarter instead of harder, and so that you end up achieving your ultimate goal of financial freedom.

So think of your real estate investing business like an NFL owner would think about his or her team. If you want to succeed in the NFL, you need the best of the best working with you. Your real estate business is no different. This is *your life* and your *financial wellbeing* we are talking about, so make sure you assemble the best team possible. The advisors you create relationships with will have a dramatic impact and influence on your long-term success.

Let's talk about the individuals you'll want to put on your advisory team.

REAL ESTATE COACHES

Of all your team members, these individuals are the most important. They will be the ones who provide the strategy and business model that you will want to follow. Rather than just blindly trying to build a real estate investing business, you will rely on them for strategic advice so you accomplish significantly more in a much shorter period of time. Ultimately, these coaches will be the people you work with most closely.

Of course, there are many different sectors of real estate, so having a team of experts is the best approach. For example, suppose you're working on a wholesale deal and the seller wants your deposit to be nonrefundable. At that point you'd better know you have a great deal at a great price that you can wholesale. You should have a more experienced second set of eyes looking at your deal or else you might end up losing a lot of money.

Ideally, you want to receive advice from a specialist in a specific area of real estate— in this case, an experienced investor who has bought hundreds of properties in the past. So your advisory team should be made up of real estate coaches who each have a specialty; combined, they cover the many different sectors of real estate.

MARKETING MENTORS

Learning how to market successfully is not something that came naturally to me. After completing my very first flip it took me two months to find my next deal, because I didn't have an understanding of how to create a marketing system. I hadn't realized the importance that consistent marketing played in bringing in deal flow; that's when my partners and I decided it'd be in our best interest to find specialized coaches who could teach us to market ourselves on platforms other than Match.com.

My business partners and I found ourselves attending many marketing seminars, both offline and online, and we eventually recruited two mentors—highly successful marketers who helped us grow our business immediately. We came to understand that marketing was the lifeblood of our business and it didn't matter how much we knew about real estate if we didn't have any deals to analyze and on which to make offers.

NEGOTIATION AND SALES MENTORS

They say that in life you don't get what you want; you get what you negotiate. When I first started wholesaling, I didn't understand how valuable this skill set would be and how much it could affect the profitability of a deal.

There are literally tens of thousands of dollars at stake on an average $200,000 property. That is not even taking into consideration the price you pay for the property, which is obviously the most critical negotiation. When you wholesale a property, you can negotiate everything from the price you pay, to the cost of money you borrow, to closings costs, and ultimately the price the buyer pays for the deal.

This is why it is essential to develop your communication, persuasion, and sales skills as an investor. When I started buying and selling houses, I didn't have a clue how essential these skill sets would be. Over time, I became more conscious of the fact that I needed to learn how to sell, because I had never held a position previously where sales skills were required. I knew it would take time to develop these skills, so I attended seminars and paid sales trainers to work with me.

I have also invested significantly in sales and communications training for employees within my real estate office. In real estate, you are constantly selling yourself—whether you are working with an agent, contractor, seller, or buyer. It is an essential skill and a craft you should always be working on. You will see immediate changes in your profitability when you take the time to receive mentoring in these areas of real estate.

BUSINESS MANAGEMENT MENTORS

Buying and selling real estate and understanding the mechanics of how real estate deals are done is one thing. Learning how to run, grow, and scale a business is something completely different. This is why I highly recommend you only mentor under people who understand both.

Personally, I saw a dramatic jump in revenue when I hired my first business coach years ago. My coach, who was not so caught up in day-to-day activities, easily identified problems that I could not see. He had a different way of looking at things from the outside, and immediately I began making huge strides. My coach helped me to be much more strategic with my time, which is probably the single biggest gift he gave me.

I began to outsource many of the mundane marketing activities that were consuming big chunks of time. Upon my coach's advice, I also built and implemented a back-end database to track all of our contacts, leads, offers, and transactions. This saved everyone vast amounts of time every day. We also started tracking the financials of our business, which resulted in well over six figures of additional profit the same year.

Much like my athletic coaches, my business coach was leading me on a set path that resulted in more time freedom from my business.

LEGAL MENTORS

Naively, my business partners and I thought early on that we could use one attorney for all of our business matters and real estate deal–related matters. We quickly realized this is not the case. The best attorneys usually specialize in one or two areas of law.

We now have a variety of legal specialists who advise us on everything from asset protection, business law, contract law, employment law, eviction law, and planning and zoning law to litigation. Specialists who can give you the best advice can literally save your business from disaster.

TAX MENTORS

Whether you like it or not, you have a silent partner on every single real estate transaction you complete. Your partner is the IRS. It goes without saying that taxes are a good thing, except when you are paying them. As mentioned before, my partners and I learned that we needed a tax specialist on our team after our first full year of business, which was also when it was too late to do any advance tax planning. A lot of our profits were tied up in other deals, and our tax bill was enormous. I remember thinking, "How the heck are we going to pay that?"

Luckily, we were able to pay the tax bill without incurring any interest; however, forking over that cash was a very valuable lesson on why we needed to find a tax specialist. Little did we know that there are some very easy ways to reduce and defer your tax liability as a real estate investor. But you don't know what you don't know, right?

Obtaining tax advice from your Uncle Larry who owns his own pizza joint and likes to hide the dough is probably not the best idea; I highly recommend you find and start building relationships with multiple strategic advisors. Remember, you don't have to know it all—you just have to assemble a team of people who know it all. It may take time to find the right people, but keep asking other investors, networking, and evaluating until you find the right fit for your team.

MASTERMIND GROUP

My business partner is a highly skeptical person. He is the type of person who needs to see something to believe it; meanwhile, I've always been the type to jump on a big opportunity and hope I'm not proven wrong. Years ago, when I decided to invest a considerable amount of money to join a mastermind group that only had two one-day meetings over the course of a year, he questioned my thought process.

However, we both realized after participating in that group that it was one of the best decisions we had ever made as business owners. In that first mastermind group and others we have joined since then, we have created strong business relationships with some of the brightest real estate investors in the country.

A good mastermind group is usually made up of peers in your industry who are trying to achieve very similar goals with their businesses. It is a group of people with whom you can brainstorm and share best industry practices. It is the collective genius of the people within the group that makes the group so valuable. In any group, there will be people with a wide variety of backgrounds and experiences, who with one suggestion or idea can help you completely change your business.

Ideally, you want other real estate investors in your mastermind group who do business in other markets around the country. When members of the group live in other markets, they are often more open about what's really working and are open to sharing best practices. Preferably, you meet with your group a couple times a year so you can continue to build and foster the relationships within the group. One relationship or one idea is all it takes to make a mastermind group worthwhile, regardless of the investment. You will always find a variety of solid skill sets in a diverse group.

CONCLUSION

Our team of strategic advisors is the reason why my business partners and I have been able to grow our investing business so quickly. Over the years, being able to pick up the phone and call people that have specialized knowledge has been an invaluable resource for us. Take the time to really ask yourself whether you have the best advisory team for your business. If you don't, rebuilding the support team you need is something that deserves your focus right away.

With your business advisory team in place, you will have a much higher probability of building a successful real estate business. In the final chapter, I present strategies for growing your business and increasing your level of personal freedom.

CHAPTER 31

The Path of Smart Growth

Intellectual growth should commence at birth and cease only at death.

—ALBERT EINSTEIN

At the end of the road, you find yourself back at square one: following your *why*. To grow your business successfully, you need to know where you ultimately want to go. Maybe investing is your passion and you want to keep expanding the business. Maybe you want to remove yourself from the business so that you can spend more time pursuing other things.

Whatever the case, the path that takes you there is going to be to a *transition*. You are going to transform your investing business from a model that is dependent on you to one that is dependent on systems and other people. And in order to achieve that goal, you need to have a path to growth that makes sense.

This chapter takes you through the steps of expanding and eventually removing yourself from your business so that you can lead it down the path of smart growth.

PREPARING FOR GROWTH

For your business to grow into one that is not dependent on you as the business owner, you must go from the phase of working *in* the business to that of working *on* the business.

When you first start out you are going to be in the field, learning, creating the systems, and improving the processes. You will then be able to hand those systems off to an employee and step into the role of manager. In order to truly remove yourself from the business, as your departments develop, you'll hire managers to take over those roles as well. You will then have stepped into the role of a true entrepreneur.

I often find investors who want to get to that level and yet are reluctant to let go of the day-to-day tasks within their business. These investors end up becoming their own biggest barriers to success. First, you must believe that you can and will build a successful business that will not be dependent on you. Then you must be willing to take action to create this as your own reality.

MANAGING YOUR TIME

As a real estate investor and entrepreneur, time is your most valuable asset. The most successful investors are the ones who are usually the most focused and effective with their time. If time is truly our most valuable asset, we'd better organize, manage, and invest it. Here are some important elements of time management.

The first step in learning how to better leverage your time is to see where you currently use it. Start by keeping a detailed journal of how you spend your time over the course of a few days. Record what you do in 15-minute increments. This will give you a snapshot of how you use your time so that you can begin the process of valuing, controlling, outsourcing, and eventually owning your time.

The second step is to divide your day into blocks of assigned time that allow you to focus on a specific activity or area of your business. In the office, I post my time-block schedule outside my door so that people know when not to interrupt me. Try programming your time-block schedule into an application like Google calendar that will notify you 10 minutes before you're supposed to switch activities.

The third step is to limit your daily goals. Being busy may look good, but it's often used to avoid the few critically important but uncomfortable projects that need to get done. Get the most out of your time by limiting your daily goals so that you stay focused on the things that really matter.

The final step is to apply the 80/20 rule. Your time and focus should always be spent on income-generating activities for your business. List all the activities you do in your business and highlight the top 20 percent of them that contribute to increasing revenues. Then examine the other 80 percent of activities to see what can be outsourced.

These time-management strategies will help you grow a business that requires less of your time and allows you to design the life of your dreams. Even if it's tedious at first, keep your eye on the prize; it's a small sacrifice to make to build a long-term profitable business in which you own your time.

DEVELOPING SYSTEMS

If you want to enjoy your life outside of real estate, then you have to develop a systems-dependent business. Your goal as a business owner should be to set up and automate common business processes by putting a system in place. When you do this it allows you to spend subsequently less time on each individual transaction.

Systemization is the process of reducing complex activities into organized processes. Systems are the foundation on which your business can grow. They provide accountability and measurability, they ensure consistency and quality control, and they allow work to happen in an efficient and timely manner while reducing the rate of human error.

The core operating system of your business should be made up of three critical functions that must all work together seamlessly: lead generation, lead conversion, and client fulfillment. Steps of the wholesaling process that can benefit from systems include taking leads, evaluating properties, writing contracts, financing, finding the buyer, and closing the deal. With systems in place, you can run your business without actually running your business.

GROWING AT A SUSTAINABLE PACE

The most dangerous real estate investors I've seen are the ones who try to take on too much, too quickly. Overconfidence has crushed many real estate investors who had a lot of potential, but grew too quickly. I know of a few investors who went from literally completing their third or fourth deal to trying to manage multiple wholesale and rehab deals at the same time. Then they made a mistake that led to another mistake and the whole house of cards came crumbling down on them.

Don't try to grow too quickly. Ideally, you want your business to grow at a steady and sustainable pace as you put your systems in place. This is also why your path of growth must be steady and planned out. You need to know that you have the systems, staff, technology, and capital in place to handle the increasing number of projects. That's the kind of growth that gets you to your goals and turns your long-term business vision into a reality.

INTEGRATING TECHNOLOGY INTO YOUR BUSINESS MANAGEMENT SYSTEMS

Leveraging the right technology is another necessary step on your path to smart growth. It is imperative to leverage the right technology not only for where you are right now, but also for where you are looking to go. Technology can help you to keep track of what is going on within your business. It eases the flow of communication, and it is a good, quick place to store various amounts of information. Throughout this book I have discussed the importance of having a trophy database and a strong back-end business management system.

The lack of a centralized database and the inability to follow up with clients is one of the top reasons why so many investors struggle and never grow their business beyond the one-deal-at-a-time outfit. This is why I highly advise every investor to have a good Client Relationship Management (CRM) system that has *e-mail marketing functionality*. These two pieces of technology are essential to your long-term success.

Don't fear technology. Embrace it as a necessary part of growth, and allow it to help you take your business to the next level.

HIRING EMPLOYEES AND SCALING YOUR BUSINESS

As a real estate investor, people are your greatest asset. The people you choose are your army, and it's important to choose well. If your goal is to build a business that is not dependent on you, hiring employees is one of the most important decisions you will ever make.

Selecting the right people actually starts before you hire your first employee. There are many people on your team, such as mortgage brokers, Realtors, and closing attorneys, who can make or break a deal. Seeking out and retaining the best of the best in these fields in your area will not only help you from transaction to transaction, it will help grow your business.

When you do start hiring, you want to recruit your "A-team." Your ideal candidates should have the following qualities: problem solvers, passion, resourcefulness, team players, track record, integrity, and great communication. Then, after you find good people, give them good instructions. Develop an IDP—an *individual development plan*—for each position at your company that your new hires can use. The IDP should contain a detailed description of the employee's role at the company, and every person you hire should have one.

Once you have your A-team assembled, do everything you can to create a culture of likeminded individuals working toward the same goals with the same mindset. When you do this, people get excited to come to the office every day.

And finally, just like systems and technology, we invest in improving our team members as well. The more knowledge, experience, and responsibility they gain, the more valuable they become to the team and the more the business can develop as a whole.

Remember, education is a journey, not a destination, and this philosophy should be lived by every one of the members on your team.

Hiring the right people as you begin to build a team will help your business grow astronomically. It will also make scaling your business and reaching your goals a heck of a lot easier. Take your time when making a hiring decision. You'll waste far more time and energy firing a bad hire within a few months, than if you just took the time to identify, interview, rate, and hire the right person to begin with.

CONSTANTLY IMPROVING YOUR LEADERSHIP SKILLS

The path of smart growth is about being strategic. It's about putting focus on the areas of your business that will push you to the ultimate success you're looking for as quickly as you can reasonably get there. And it's about being balanced in how you grow. By working on the areas of your business that need to be improved—systems, technology, building a team, or anything else that factors in as your weakest link—you are positioning yourself for long-term sustainable growth.

Any team, no matter how strong it is, will only go as far as you lead it. All teams need strong leaders in order to reach their full potential. As the leader of your business, you personally have to embrace personal development by constantly improving on your own set of skills. When you do, that same spirit of growth and learning will filter through your entire organization, inspiring a culture of never-ending improvement.

Building a business is not easy. If it were, everyone would do it. As a real estate investor, you will be challenged mentally, physically, and emotionally. You will learn more about yourself than you ever expected, and you will be better off because of it. And, if you're anything like me, you wouldn't have it any other way.

Enjoy the journey.

Index

240

INDEX